MISCARRIAGES OF
JUSTICE

BLITZ EDITIONS

Published by Blitz Editions
an imprint of Bookmart Ltd
Registered Number 2372865
Trading as Bookmart Ltd
Desford Road
Enderby
Leicester LE9 5AD

ISBN 1 85605 137 4

This material has previously appeared in *Murder and Madness*.

Every effort has been made to contact the copyright holders for the pictures.
In some cases they have been untraceable, for which we offer our apologies.
Special thanks to the Hulton-Deutsch Collection, who supplied the majority of pictures,
and thanks also to the following libraries and picture agencies:
Press Association, Frank Spooner Pictures, Syndication International

Designed by COOPER WILSON DESIGN

MISCARRIAGE OF JUSTICE

THE GUILDFORD 4 & BIRMINGHAM 6

These IRA atrocities horrified and enraged Britons who demanded instant and terrible punishment. In the name of justice, the police became as corrupt as the men they hunted. How were the wrong men imprisoned and where are the real killers?

Justice stands blindfolded over the Old Bailey in London, Britain's highest criminal court. She also stands tarnished in many people's eyes after a series of miscarriages of justice that deeply shook the ingrained faith of the British people in the equality and fairness of their country's judicial system. With the overturning on appeal of convictions against supposed IRA terrorists in the case of the Guildford and Birmingham pub bombings, the system that is admired the world over was shown to be deeply flawed.

Ten people, totally innocent, languished in jails for many years, their pleas of innocence not believed, the testimony against them thin at best and fabricated at worst. Victims of a deep-rooted national need to punish anyone for the outrages that left innocent civilians dead, these unfortunates paid the price in the witch-hunt that followed each bombing. Only by learning the lessons from each case can Britain hope to restore the lustre to the lady with the scales on top of Old Bailey.

THE GUILDFORD FOUR

Guildford is a quintessentially English town, a Surrey oasis of green, with quaint pubs and neat houses set in the suburban London sprawl. But in October 1974 five people died in two of those quaint pubs, the Horse and Groom, and the Seven Stars. Massive bombs, one a 'missile' device,

shattered the bars and claimed the lives of the innocent people, wounding thirty-five, some seriously, in the process. Both pubs were often used by army guardsmen from barracks at nearby Pirbright and Aldershot. A month later, on 7 November, a massive explosion at the King's Arms pub in Woolwich – long an army arsenal with

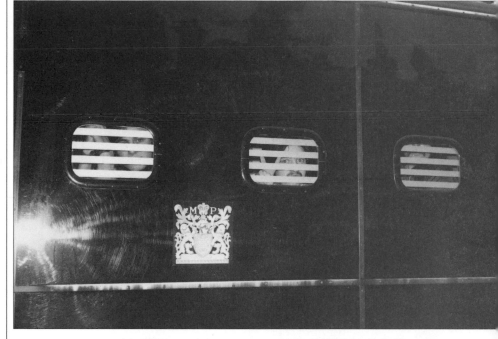

numerous garrisons – claimed two more lives and injured many more. The Irish Republican Army's assault on the British mainland was being stepped up.

Since 1969, when the Provisional IRA leadership was re-formed, with the hardliners winning office. The avowed aim of the organisation was to bomb, shoot, murder the British out of Ulster. The Seventies were to be the inglorious decade of the terrorist in the world and Britain was not spared. However, bombing pubs and so killing people like twenty-one-year-old secretary Jillian Johnston, when she was enjoying a drink with friends, with her whole life stretched before her, did not intimidate the British. Such acts did not alter government policies. The outrages served only to strengthen the national contempt of such barbarians – and created a climate in which hatred would eventually pervert the course of British justice.

In the months before the bombing an IRA active service unit was officially formed in London. It had a long list of potential targets and a supply of bomb

Above: *Victory signs can be glimpsed through the bars of the police van as the Guildford Four are driven away during their re-trial.*

Opposite: *Gerry Conlon is led from the Old Bailey after his release from false imprisonment.*

TEN PEOPLE, TOTALLY INNOCENT, LANGUISHED IN JAILS FOR MANY YEARS, THEIR PLEAS OF INNOCENCE NOT BELIEVED, THE TESTIMONY AGAINST THEM THIN.

Below: *The Guildford Four were naturally jubilant at their release after many years in prison for crimes they did not commit. Their families had also had their lives blighted.*

making materials hidden at various points on the mainland. Shortly after the arrival of this murder team came Belfast-born Gerry Conlon and his girlfriend Eileen McCann. They came to England to seek work in August and were joined later that month by Paul Hill, his sister Elizabeth and his girlfriend Gina Clarke. In London, they would later meet Paddy Armstrong, an Irish dropout with a drug problem who lived in a squat in Kilburn, North London, he shared with his girlfriend Carole Richardson. In the mania to find culprits for the hideous crimes of the active service unit, Hill, Conlon, Armstrong and Richardson would soon be charged and would go down in criminal history as the Guildford Four.

Conlon was a petty thief, a gambler, a bit of a drunkard by his own admission, who liked to steal solely in order to pay for his pleasures. He was regarded by the IRA in his native Belfast as unsuitable for service because of his thieving. He got the money for the trip to Britain from the Criminal Injuries Compensation Board – the sum of £200 for being stabbed in a Belfast disco in a fight over a girl. Once in Britain he linked up with Hill, his old schoolfriend from Belfast, and the pair eventually lodged together in a Catholic boarding house in Kilburn. Paddy Armstrong had had a drug problem for years. Also from Ireland, he was badly down on his luck, and was living in squalor with Carole, an English girl who had first used drugs when she was only eleven. This misfit team were convicted of being an elite IRA unit.

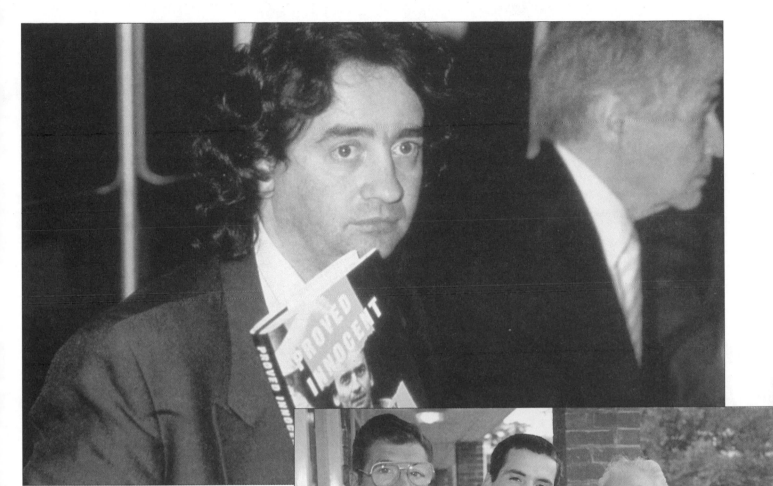

When they were arrested, the Guildford Four were the first people who, under the terms of the recently-imposed Prevention of Terrorism Act, were denied the right to have a lawyer present during interrogation. This Act was aimed at eliminating IRA activities. When the four went to court they were convicted solely on their confessions; there was not one supporting piece of forensic or other physical evidence linking them with the bombings. Consequently, when they retracted their confessions in court the prosecution mocked them and the jury believed they were liars. The Guildford Four said that their confessions has been beaten out of them; that the police officers who interrogated them behaved with all the finesse of wartime Germany's Gestapo, or so the accused claimed.

Conlon was in Belfast when he was arrested. It took fifteen years for a British newspaper to publish this account of his seizure. He said: 'They were slapping me all over the place. My clothes were covered in blood and my family had to bring clean ones for me. At Heathrow things got worse. The station was cold and frightening. There

was a reception committee. There must have been around twenty-five policemen all crowding round me, all glaring and shouting things like "you Irish bastard". They made me take off my clothes in front of them all and they made some sarcastic comments. Some were spitting on me.

'They took me down to a cell. All it had in it was a wooden bench. I was like that until twelve o'clock the next day. People kept coming down to look at me like some

Above: *Sean Smyth, Patrick Maguire, Paddy Maguire and Ann Maguire. The Maguire family fought long and hard to prove their relatives were innocent.*

Top: *Gerry Conlon holds his book 'Proven Innocent' which is a document of his experience.*

animal in a zoo. I was interrogated for two days. I couldn't believe police officers, people who are supposed to be serious, intelligent people, could go down to that level. I couldn't believe anyone could go off the handle like they did. Two officers were particularly hard on me. One said he would show me an old RAF trick. He put his hands behind my ears and pulled me up off the chair. It was very painful.

'Another senior man was more aggressive verbally than physically but he slapped

'THREATS FROM A SENIOR SURREY CID OFFICER MADE ME SIGN TWO CONFESSIONS. HE TOLD ME AN ACCIDENT COULD BE ARRANGED FOR MY MOTHER AND MY SISTER.'

According to the other three, there was similar treatment for them. In fear, Conlon was named by Hill, who was the first to be arrested in November 1974. The others were named by Conlon. The police were now eager to clear up the bombing. At the trial at the Old Bailey in 1975 there was no mercy; all accused were sentenced to life on the strength of their confessions. Hill and Conlon were convicted separately of the bombing at Woolwich and received life sentences in relation to that crime. They

me in the face, wagged his finger and pulled my nose. He told me, he assured me, that I would make a statement. It seemed they would do anything to convict me. They were under enormous pressure from the Press and the television. Threats from a senior Surrey CID officer made me sign two confessions. He told me an accident could be arranged for my mother and my sister. He told me that if a soldier shot my mother it would be put down to an accident and British soldiers were never convicted in the courts. That's when it became a whole different thing. I knew he could probably do what he said.'

Above: *Paddy Hill takes the microphone to proclaim his release. He is one of the Birmingham Six.*

Opposite, above: *Paddy McIlkenny waves jubilantly as he walks to freedom.*

Opposite, below: *Gerry Conlon, of the Birmingham Four, arrives at court with Maggie McIlkenny, daughter of Paddy, to listen to her father's appeal.*

appealed in 1977 – an appeal that was rejected. Meanwhile the true active service unit of the IRA continued to create mayhem on the British mainland.

It was at the trial of this terror squad in early 1977, the terrorists having been caught after a siege in London's Balcombe Street, that one of the men read out a statement. These terrorists were the core of the active-service unit and they were cornered after shooting up a restaurant in Mayfair. But they escaped and held a couple hostage for six days in a siege with police in an apartment at Balcombe Street, Marylebone before they finally gave themselves up.

In part the statement read: 'We are all four Irish Republicans. We have recognised this court to the extent that we have instructed our lawyers to draw the attention of the court to the fact that four totally innocent people – Carole Richardson, Gerard Conlon, Paul Hill and Patrick Armstrong – are serving massive sentences for three bombings, two in Guildford and one in Woolwich which three of us and another man now imprisoned have admitted that we did. The Director of Public Prosecutions was made aware of these admissions in December 1975 and has chosen to do nothing.' Was this true?

A LIMITED APPEAL

When the Guildford Four went to the appeal court to have the Balcombe Street siege gang's confessions put before a new jury at a fresh trial, the judges heard evidence in person by the self-confessed bombers. However, the court decided, on the evidence that was given, that both the Balcombe Street Siege gang and the Guildford Four were responsible for the

THE COURT DECIDED THAT BOTH THE BALCOMBE STREET SIEGE GANG AND THE GUILDFORD FOUR WERE GUILTY.

bombings. No controversy about forensic evidence of the authenticity of police reports,were raised during this appeal.

Even before this, early in 1975, the Director of Public Prosecutions received two secret Scotland Yard reports that cast serious doubts on the guilty verdicts handed down on the Guildford Four. One document was prepared shortly before and the

Above: *The Birmingham Six greet well-wishers as they leave the court that granted their appeal.*

THESE SECRET REPORTS SUGGESTED THAT ALL THE EVIDENCE POINTED AWAY FROM, NOT TOWARDS, THE GUILDFORD FOUR.

other shortly after the convictions. Essentially, the documents chronicled the IRA terror campaign on the mainland, linking incidents both before and after the four were arrested. This meant that someone else was doing the killing. One of the police reports said that there appeared to be a 'common thread and purpose' between the Guildford attacks and other IRA bombings in Britain. The reports could find no link between the convicted four and the IRA – and no physical evidence to suggest they did it. They were sent down on confessions made under duress.

These secret reports, which suggested that all evidence pointed away from, not towards, the Guildford Four, were adequate testimony to spare the innocents their fifteen years in prison. When these documents were made public, in 1989, Alistair Logan, a solicitor who represented two of the Guildford Four, said: 'The reports clearly show that the police knew the bombings at Guildford were linked to other bombings. I had no idea at the time that the police had this evidence. It is shocking.' Why did the police hide these documents?

MORE NAMES, MORE REPORTS

The second police report was written after conviction of the four, in December 1975, and it named Joseph Patrick Gilhooley as a senior IRA man involved in mainland terror operations. Gilhooley is suspected as the third man involved in the Guildford pub bombings along with Balcombe Street siege terrorisst Joseph O'Connell, and Brendan Dowd, who was arrested in the north of England early in 1975 for terrorist offences. O'Connell and Dowd always refused to name this accomplice, or two women who helped them plant the bombs. However, there is a suspicion that Gilhooley was involved in the Guildford bombings but there is no evidence to support this.

For the Guildford Four, the years passed, slowly and painfully. They alledged they were beaten up in various jails – the general prison population has never been overly friendly to child molestors or terrorists. Although the families of the men kept up a constant campaign, it seemed as if justice truly was blind to their case.

Even so, the four attracted a significant clique of wealthy and influential people to their cause: former Home Secretaries Roy Jenkins and Merlyn Rees, former Law Lords Devlin and Scarman, and the Archbishop of Westminster Cardinal Basil Hume. These men were concerned exclusively with new evidence that had turned up in the years since the bombing. Richardson and Armstrong had witnesses to say that they were in a pub in the Elephant and Castle in South London on the night of the bombing, while Hill had a witness to testify that he was in the hostel. In April 1989, lawyers for Conlon discovered that a witness vital to their client's case whom they had been unable to trace had been interviewed by Surrey dectectives in 1975 – a crucial part of the investigation that was never submitted at the trial yet would have given Conlon an alibi.

The Home Secretary Douglas Hurd ordered an inquiry to be conducted into the Surrey police handling of the case in 1989. Officers of the Somerset and Avon force gave their disturbing findings to Sir

> THE FOUR ATTRACTED A SIGNIFICANT CLIQUE OF WEALTHY AND INFLUENTIAL PEOPLE TO THEIR CAUSE.

Below: *Smiles of relief and happiness were on the faces of every one of the Six as they drove off to re-start their lives.*

Partrick Mayhew, the Attorney General, who in turn passed them on to Mr Hurd in October. It was bad news for the government; the police probers had found evidence of the initial Scotland Yard reports, the dismissal of the alibi witness so important to Conlon and numerous allegations of brutality towards the suspects. Hurd had no choice but to report before Parliament that the case would be going back before the Court of Appeal.

A CRY FOR FREEDOM

When the four were brought before the judges at the court where they were sentenced, they were informed that the Crown had withdrawn all charges against them and that they were free. On 19 October 1989, they walked out to a crowd whose cheers that echoed from the rooftops around the Old Bailey.

Paul Hill was thirty-four; Richardson, thirty-two; Conlon, thirty-four; and Armstrong, thirty-nine. It was time to rebuild their lives with the compensation money due to them, but who can really put a price on fourteen years in prison? Nothing can give them back the lost time.

THE BIRMINGHAM SIX

For the men wrongly accused of the murder of twenty-one people in the worst IRA carnage on mainland Britain, there were sixteen agonising years in jail, served for offences they didn't commit. The Birmingham Six, unlike the Guildford Four, had Republican sympathies which weighed against them at their trial – and there was forensic evidence (since discredited) that seemed at the time to point to them. Their conviction was further proof that some police tailored evidence while under intense pressure to find those guilty of a crime that stunned the nation.

The Tavern in the Town and Mulberry Bush pubs in Birmingham, in the heart of the city, were obliterated on the night of 21 November 1974, and with them any lingering tolerance that certain sections of society may have harboured for the IRA and their aims. In the appalling carnage that killed twenty-one innocents, a further one hundred and sixty-two were injured, many of them seriously. The scenes of devastation looked like something hit in the London Blitz at its worst. One of the pubs was underground, making the explosion that much more effective. Some of the victims were literally blown to smithereens. In the aftermath of the bomb-

*Top: **Families discuss proceedings during the appeal hearing.***

*Above and right: **Paddy Hill, above, and John Walker, right, innocent men wrongly convicted.***

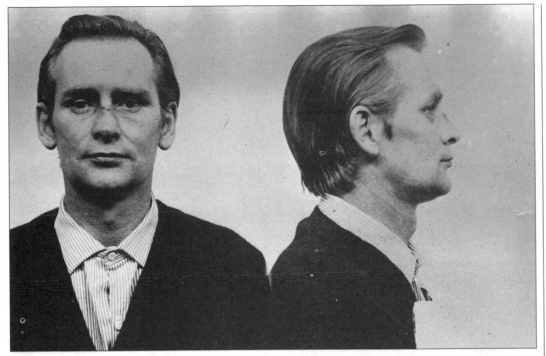

ONE OF THE PUBS WAS UNDERGROUND, MAKING THE EXPLOSION THAT MUCH MORE EFFECTIVE. SOME OF THE VICTIMS WERE LITERALLY BLOWN TO SMITHEREENS.

ings, grief was soon followed by angry cries of vengeance. The public demanded that the Birmingham pub massacres were avenged and the guilty men caught and punished for their dreadful crimes of terror and the murder of innocent people.

The West Midlands police force was given responsibility for tracking down the IRA team. The usual trawl of suspects began with heightened surveillance at air and sea ports. Police infiltrated the Irish communities of Birmingham and Liverpool. The law officers were all too aware of the public desire for a swift and total conclusion to the terrorist crimes.

Detectives couldn't believe their luck when they intercepted the party of six men heading for the ferry in Liverpool that was sailing to Ireland the next morning; the men were on their way to the funeral of an IRA bomber and had come from the West Midlands area. The men were named as John Walker, Patrick Hill, Hugh Callaghan, Richard McIlkenny, Gerard Hunter and William Power. Like the Guildford Four, they were interviewed without solicitors present and the interviews were not tape recorded, as is now required by law. There were

confessions from the men – confessions obtained, it was admitted sixteen long years later, by police methods that were entirely unacceptable. The Birmingham Six claimed that the only way to stop the police beating and threatening them was to sign false confessions, the confessions that were used as evidence at their trial.

But for the Birmingham Six there was also forensic evidence against them. Tests carried out on the men showed that at least two of them had minute traces of nitroglyc-

Richard McIlkenny (above) and Hugh Callaghan (below) as they were when they went to prison for a crime neither committed.

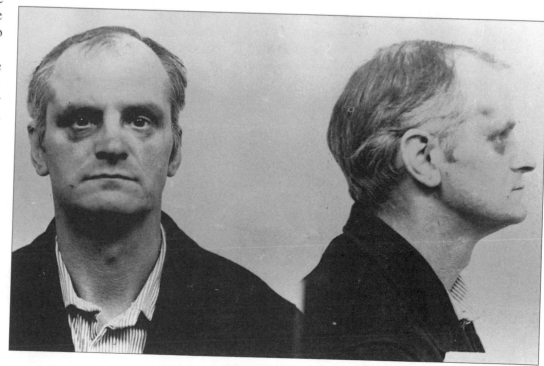

erine on their hands. It was enough for them to be convicted at Lancaster Crown Court where Mr Justice Bridge, sentencing them to life prison terms, said: 'You stand convicted on each of twenty-one counts, on the clearest and most overwhelming evidence I have ever heard, of the crime of murder. I am entirely satisfied that the investigations were carried out with scrupulous propriety by all officers.' The men descended to the cells, their pleas of innocence lost on a court that had unwittingly accepted false evidence. It seemed, at the time, to be a fair trial based on scientific proof of guilt.

ANOTHER TRIAL FOR THE LAW

It was in 1985, ten years after they were sentenced, that a Granada 'World in Action' programme began to seriously

Above: *The aftermath to the bombing in Birmingham.*

question the convictions. Chris Mullin, the Labour MP, became one of their unstinting supporters, despite the hatred still directed at the accused by a public unaware of the dishonest police role. Politicians in the Irish Republic began demand a review of the trial and the verdicts, as did the Roman Catholic Archbishop of Birmingham, who several times called into question the validity of their convictions. But after the release of the Guildford Four, the public began to suspect the police role in the Birmingham Six affair, and a final and successful review of their convictions was ordered by the Home Secretary.

Forensic science technology, which played a considerable part in the conviction of the men, also contributed in a major way to their freedom. The six were incriminated initially by a scientific test designed in the 1860s by Johann Peter Griess. Most explosives contain nitrogen and the Griess test detects nitrogen-containing chemicals (nitrites) which can be liberated from explosives when they are treated with alkali solutions. Interpretation in the testing is critical – anything which contains nitrite or something that can be converted to it will produce a positive result. Essentially, a scientist must be extremely cautious when examining test results to ensure that he has detected the right kind of nitrites. At the trial, Home Office scientist Dr Frank Skuse testified that the Griess test given to William Power and Patrick Hill made him 'ninety-nine per cent certain' that they had handled nitroglycerine, the explosive used in the bombs. But it was later learned that common household soap could produce the same chemical result.

Another explosives test was done – the gas chromatography/mass spectrometry test, regarded as more sensitive and more reliable. But the trace used for the test was later found to be too small – it could easily have come from the tobacco residue on a

> 'I AM ENTIRELY SATISFIED THAT THE INVESTIGATIONS WERE CARRIED OUT WITH SCRUPULOUS PROPRIETY BY ALL OFFICERS.'

Below: *Police and rescue workers discuss strategy after the bombing in Birmingham.*

cigarette smoker's hand. In appeal evidence, Home Office scientist Dr Alan Scaplehorn agreed that the test, in regard to the positive nitroglycerine traces found on Hill's hands, was 'not acceptable'.

Advanced machinery in the form of an electrostatic document analysis apparatus supported part of their appeal. Police claimed that material in their notebooks was written as interrogations were taking place. The electrostatic document analysis process proved them wrong. The ESDA machine proved that four different pads and inks were used in nineteen pages covering two interviews – suggesting they were completed at different times.

At the appeal in 1991, Mr Michael Mansfield, their QC, said the discrepancies were part of an 'intricate web of deceit' involving a pattern of altered timings and later insertions. The tests were conducted in 1990 by officers from Devon and Cornwall police who were given the task by the Home Office of investigating the convictions. It was after the results of the

Above: *The Birmingham Six from left to right: top, Patrick Hill, Hugh Callaghan, John Walker; lower row, Richard McIlkenny, Gerry Hunter and Billy Power.*

forensic evidence that the Director of Public Prosecutions decided that he could no longer believe that police reports on interviews with the men were accurate or truthful. In short, there was no longer a case for them to answer.

Older and greyer, robbed of the best years of their lives, the six walked into the street outside Old Bailey on 14 March 1991, their ordeal over, the lost and wasted years a tragic but ever-present memory. Families had been deprived of their husbands and fathers. A deafening cheer went up as they emerged as free men for the first time in sixteen years, their supporters mobbing them as police fought to keep a path clear for them. The six – McIlkenny, fifty-seven; Callaghan, sixty; Hill, forty-five; Hunter, forty-two; Power, forty-four; and Walker, fifty-five – were all naturally bitter.

Patrick Hill said to wild applause outside the court: 'For sixteen years we have been political scapegoats. Police said to us from the start that they knew we had not done it but they told us they did not care. We were selected and they were going to frame us for it to keep everybody happy.' Hugh Callaghan said: 'Justice has been done today. It has taken sixteen years for it to happen. Thank you very much.'

'WE ARE LEFT WITH NOTHING'

For the victims of the bombers – the real bombers, who have never been brought to trial – there was only a hollow emptiness left. Ivy Roberts, whose daughter Maureen was among the dead, said: 'There was some compensation in knowing that the guilty men were in jail, but now we are left with nothing. The families of the dead have had to live with this every day since the bombings. But the victims appear to have been forgotten by others. If they did not plant those bombs somebody else did. Are the police now going to bring them to justice?' Mrs Elizabeth Gray, sixty-eight, is also horrified that the guilty men are still free. Having lost her brother-in-law Charles in the Mulberry Bush explosion, she said: 'At the time we thought they had got the right men but mistakes can be made. There were terrible doubts, I now know, from the beginning. The men's families must have suffered terribly. But whoever did it is free and that sickens me.'

There are now calls for reforms of the judicial system and a Royal Commission was charged, after the success of the appeal, with reviewing the entire process. But it will, in all likelihood, be several years before any reforms can be implemented. In the meantime, the murderers of twenty-one innocent people remain free and the six people who were accused of killing the victims are left to pick up the remains of their shattered lives.

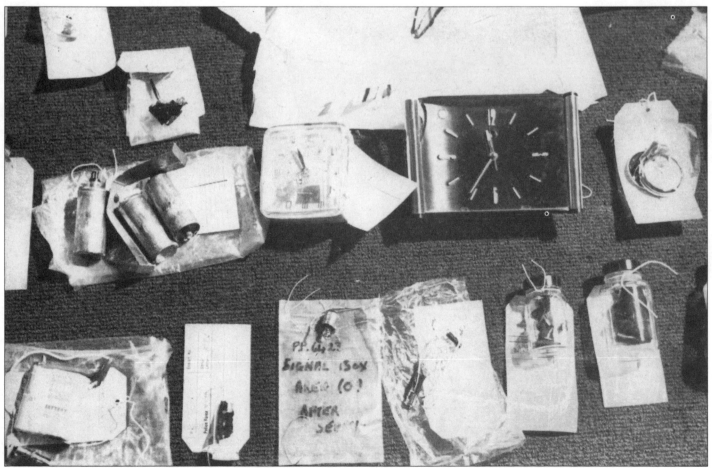

JAMES HANRATTY
The Wrong A6 Murderer

James Hanratty was wanted for burglary but was hanged instead for the brutal A6 Murder. This sad small-time crook who insisted on his innocence was long dead when the real killer, who remains unpunished, confessed.

The mortal remains of James Hanratty have long turned to dust but his ghost will not lie down. The conviction and subsequent execution of twenty-five-year-old Hanratty for the crime known as the A6 Murder has been a subject of controversy ever since he was put to death in Bedford on 4 April 1962. Books by such eminent scholars as Lord Russell of Liverpool have cast doubt upon his guilt; more recently a television programme about the case was broadcast and campaigners seeking to have his innocence restored have pressed Scotland Yard for DNA samples for 'genetic fingerprinting' tests which could conclusively prove or disprove his involvement in the murder of Michael John Gregsten.

Hanratty was born in Wembley, Middlesex, in 1936, the eldest of four sons. He was a slow learner at school, a child who needed special attention, and he never learned much more than basic arithmetic and English. Evacuated during the height of the London Blitz, he ran with street toughs upon his return. In the post-war years he was a young man heading downwards into a life of crime.

From the age of fourteen he was a shoplifter and a car thief, graduating to his first prison sentence for housebreaking when he was eighteen. His father tried many times to get his son to go straight but it was to no avail. In 1957 he was in jail again for burglary, released at the end of the year, and imprisoned again in 1958, this time for three years. When he was freed in 1960, his father gave up his job as a dust-

man in order to start a window cleaning business with his son – a vain attempt to keep the boy out of trouble. It failed, and in the autumn of that year young Hanratty went on the run for a burglary when he knew police had him in their sights as the prime suspect. It was when he was hiding out that his underworld contacts tipped him off that he was also wanted by the police for the horrifying killing of a scientist which the papers had called the A6 Murder.

Michael Gregsten was thirty-six and enjoying a passionate affair with Valerie Storie, a twenty-three-year-old research assistant who worked with him at the Road Research Laboratory near Slough. Gregsten was married but separated from his wife. She had custody of their two small sons, he took the Morris Minor saloon car.

In the early hours of 23 August 1961 Gregsten and his girlfriend shared a few drinks together at a pub in Taplow, on the Thames not far from Slough, and then drove to one of their favourite 'courting

Below: *Obscured beneath a blanket, Hanratty arrives at court to face charges of murder. He was a petty thief but nothing in his past suggested that he was prone to violent crime and attempted murder.*

couples' spots at a nearby cornfield. It was while they were sitting in the car that a tap came on the window. Annoyed that their tryst had been interrupted, Gregsten opened it and found himself staring down the barrel of a revolver pointed straight at his face. The mystery man, his face shrouded in shadow, demanded the car keys.

Opposite: *James Hanratty may have been the victim of a monstrous frame-up.*

his own, made a frantic bid to overpower his hijacker. The man talked about tying them up and glanced at a bundle containing clothes. As Gregsten handed it over, he hurled the bag of laundry into the gunman's face, trying to knock the gun from his hand. But in that instant the gun went off twice, killing Gregsten instantly.

MURDER, RAPE AND INJURIES

Miss Storie screamed in grief and rage: 'You bastard! Why did you do that?' The gunman, obviously nervous, said he had been frightened and that he didn't mean to kill. As he calmed her down he became more emboldened and, pointing the gun at her head, made her kiss him. Then he dragged her into the back seat and raped her. Afterwards, he made her help him drag the corpse of her lover from the car. As she wept he ordered her, at gunpoint, back to the vehicle and demand she show him how the gears worked – indicating by this, that he was a man unused to driving manual gearbox cars. Then, as she went back to grieve over Gregsten's body, he shot her several times, finally kicking her body a few times in an attempt to satisfy himself that she was indeed dead.

Convinced she was, he climbed into the driving seat and drove away. She was found shortly after daybreak by a passer-by. Valerie Storie was alive but paralysed from the waist down by a bullet that had passed too close to her spinal cord.

Police were baffled by the sheer brutality of the crime. While Det-Supt Bob Acott questioned Miss Storie in hospital, the gun was found stuffed under the seat of a London bus and the car abandoned in Ilford, Essex, far from the shooting, on the other side of the capital. An Identikit picture made up from Miss Storie's description of the murderer was circulated throughout Britain. She remembered him as having brown hair and deep set brown eyes. Acott issued an appeal to landladies to report lodgers who might be lying low or who were acting in a suspicious manner.

A break in the case seemed to come when a landlord at Amersham, Buckinghamshire, reported that a man calling himself Durrant had booked himself into his residential hotel on the day after the murder and had kept himself confined

*Above: **James Hanratty as a five-year-old photographed-with his mother.***

> MISS STORIE SCREAMED IN GRIEF AND RAGE: 'YOU BASTARD! WHY DID YOU DO THAT?'

The stranger pocketed the keys and clambered into the back seat. Initially, he robbed them of money and their watches. Then he began a rambling monologue of his life, saying that he had been in remand homes, borstals and prisons. He looked menacingly at Gregsten and said he was going to put him in the boot of the car, but changed his mind after Miss Storie pleaded with him not to do so. Then his monologue suddenly ended and he passed the keys back to his captive with instructions to drive around the northern London suburbs until he was told to stop. The courting couple and their kidnapper ended up at a lay-by on the A6 at a spot called Deadman's Hill, between Luton and Bedford.

Gregsten, obviously frightened but concerned for his girlfriend's safety as much as to his room ever since. The man was checked out by Scotland Yard and found to be one Peter Louis Alphon who was a door-to-door salesman. However, with no evidence of crime against him, the police could not arrest Alphon.

Police learned that on the night of the murder Alphon was booked into the Vienna Hotel in Maida Vale, West London. There, on 11 September, a manageress was moving furniture in room twenty-four when two spent cartridge cases fell out from a tear in the side of a chair. The woman, who had already been questioned by police about her guest, gave them to detectives straight away. Ballistic tests proved beyond a shadow of a doubt that the cartridge cases were from the weapon that claimed Michael Gregsten's life. Even though Alphon had actually slept in room six of the hotel, the police were certain that he had somehow planted the cartridge cases in the other room.

Police now set about finding Alphon again in Amersham but he had vanished. Detectives were certain they had the right

Right: *Written as he faced the death sentence, Hanratty reveals a genuine concern for, and gratitude towards, his family.*

Below: *Was Hanratty the man who hitched a lift in this Morris, then killed the driver? Police examine the car for evidence after they found it abandoned.*

As dictated by inmate to R Scott off. 3/4.

In replying to this letter, please write on the envelope:—

Number 3220 Name Hanratty

Prison

Dear Mum & Dad.
I am sending this letter very hard to put together. But I am going to try very hard to do everything I can to help you to recover from the terrable shock caused by all this. I am sorry I have caused you this terrable strain both you and Dad and all the family.
You have all been so brave all the way in the case, and to show my gratitude to you all, I am going to face up to it, and am going to be a son that you and Dad can be proud of. I have not been much of a son to you in the past but Mum what I am about to say to you, comes from

man in their sights. The manager of the Vienna told lawmen that Alphon had been out till 'well after midnight' on the date of the murder and had still not returned when he, the manager, went to bed in the early hours of the morning. He also claimed that when he saw Alphon the next day he looked unshaven and dishevelled, nervous about something. Alphon, using the alias Durrant, was now a wanted man and his name released to the newspapers. Even his mother had been visited and could not provide an alibi for her son. In their first interview with him, he had told police that he had been visiting her house in Streatham, but she denied this. Alphon, aware that it would only be a matter of time before the police tracked him down, gave himself up on 22 September.

There then followed a series of identity parades in which police hoped to establish beyond a shadow of doubt that he was their man. The first was before a Mrs Dalal of Richmond, Surrey, who, on 7 September, had opened her front door to a man seeking a room in her lodging house. She claimed her attacker bound her, forced her into the bedroom, lifted up her skirt preparatory to a rape attempt and whispered: 'I am the A6 killer'. He fled when Mrs Dalal screamed and she was unharmed. When Alphon was paraded with others before her he was

Above: *These women testified at Hanratty's trial. Mary Deacon, upper picture, had dated him and Ita O'Donovan worked at the hotel where police found evidence against Hanratty.*

Opposite, top: *Hanratty leaves the court and, as on his arrival, is protected by a covering blanket.*

Opposite, below: *Cleaner Harry Brookes points to the place where the murder weapon was found hidden under a bus seat.*

picked out by her as her would-be assailant. But the hotel manager failed to point him out, as did two men who had seen Gregsten with Storie and a male passenger in his car in the early hours of the day of his death. Finally, Alphon was brought before Valerie Storie at Guy's Hospital in a line-up held at the foot of her bed. When she picked out an innocent man she shouted: 'I've made a mistake! I've made a mistake!' Alphon was released, even though his own alibi for that night was questionable to say the least.

Police then turned their attention to the guest who occupied room twenty-four, where the bullet cases were discovered, that night. It was unoccupied the night of the murder but was booked out to a man named James Ryan the previous evening. The network of underworld informers soon tipped off police that Ryan was in fact

James Hanratty, on the run from his latest bungled burglary that could have landed him behind bars for a ten-year stretch.

Police began a nationwide search for Hanratty, who heard from criminal friends before the police found him that he was wanted for the A6 killing. Hanratty was terrified; true, he had been in plenty of trouble with the law, but sex crimes and violence were definitely not his trademarks. On 5 October, nervous about his fate, he telephoned Det-Supt Acott, when he explained that he was guilty of burglary but innocent of murder, attempted murder and rape. He told Acott: 'You know that's not my scene'. He claimed to have spent the night of the murder drinking with three men in Liverpool, but that he was not prepared to come to a police station because of the burglary he had commited, that would ensure another stretch inside for him.

However, on 11 October, Hanratty was recognised by two policeman as he strolled on the seafront at Blackpool and was immediately arrested. He was on an express train to London within twenty-four hours and again an identity parade was held before Miss Storie's bed. This time she asked all the men present to say the phrase: 'Be quiet, I'm thinking,' some words used

by Gregsten's killer. When Hanratty in his broad London accent pronounced thinking 'finkin' she unhesitatingly picked him out. Hanratty was then charged formally with Michael Gregsten's murder.

Miss Storie's identification of him and the fact that the gun cartridges were found in the room he had stayed in at the Vienna Hotel seemed to be the sum total of police evidence. But even that was sketchy on closer examination; Miss Storie had said that the killer had brown eyes and brown hair, which certainly matched Alphon. Her description did not fit Hanratty, who had wide, bright blue eyes and fair hair. She changed her description of the killer eight days before Hanratty was caught. There were rumours that some policemen had fiddled with the evidence of the cartridges, but these stories remained mere speculation.

Hanratty's case was heard at Bedford Assizes in January 1962. Miss Storie's evidence was the most compelling and that which ultimately damned him. In court, she swore again he was the man who had killed Gregsten and raped her. There was further identification from two men who, even though the light was bad, claimed they saw him driving the Morris car after he had killed Gregsten and left Miss Storie for dead. Hanratty's pleadings of innocence were not helped by his refusal to state

Above: *A policeman guards bags of evidence during Hanratty's trial at bedford Assizes.*

Below: *Mr Justice Gorman is welcomed at court by the Sherrif of Bedford County.*

where he was on the night of the murder.

But then, dramatically, in the second week of the trial, he blurted out that he had been at Rhyl, North Wales, where he had stayed in a guest house. He named the guest house and the landlady, but she was unable to ascertain if he had stayed with her the night of the murder, although she said he did in fact stay at her house. This also clashed with his first statement that he had spent the night of the killing with three men in Liverpool. But if an alibi was not established, neither was a motive. Hanratty, a semi-literate who had spent all his adult life in petty thievery and housebreaking, hardly seemed a contender for murder and rape, and that committed in such an unplanned manner. Nevertheless, he was convicted and sentenced to hang. The execution was set for 4 April 1962.

As the grey light of dawn shone through the bars of his dim, grey cell on the morning of his execution, James Hanratty penned his last words on this earth to his younger brother. 'Well Mick, I am going to do my best to face the morning with courage and strength and I am sure God will give me the courage to do so. I am going to ask you to do me a small favour, that is I would like you to try to clear my name of this crime. Someone, somewhere, is responsbile for this crime and one day they will venture again and then the truth will come out and then, Mick, that will be the chance for you to step in. Well, Mick, the time is drawing near, it is almost daylight, so please look after mum and dad for me. I only wish I could have the chance all

over again. But never mind Mick, as I don't know what I have done to deserve this. But, Mick, that's fate for you... Your loving brother, Jim.'

He hanged – the last man in Britain to suffer such a fate. But the battle over his guilt or innocence has raged on.

After his death there arrived on the scene a colourful character, the son of a Belgian diplomat called Jean Justice, who had an abiding interest in the law. Like a modern-day Poirot, he was intrigued by the Hanratty case and agreed with students of crime that the evidence arraigned against him was too circumstantial to be credible. Justice subscribed to the theory that the

A TALK WITH STRANGERS, NOT POLICE

On one occasion Alphon handed to Justice a detailed account of what happened on the night of the killing – not a confession and not signed in his own hand – but an account which further re-inforced Justice's view that he was, in fact, dealing with the man who should have been in the dock. Later he taped long telephone conversations with Alphon in which the suspect displayed an inordinate amount of knowledge about the route driven by Gregsten on the night he died. Justice highlighted the fact that Alphon was, by his own admittance, a

'ON THE PHONE HE COULD WORK HIMSELF UP TO TERRIBLE FURIES – AND HE TALKED IN RIDDLES, CONTRADICTING HIMSELF AND CONSTANTLY SHIFTING THE DETAILS OF HIS STORY.'

cartridge casings were planted in his room by Alphon who was the guilty party; he had already confessed as much to the unfortunate Mrs Dalal, if her identification was correct, and the first description by Valerie Storie matched his looks. Justice approached Alphon, who was initially reluctant to see him, but soon after agreed to a meeting. They were soon meeting on a regular basis and Alphon, perhaps flattered by the attention, began dropping boastful hints indicating that he was the killer and that an innocent Hanratty had gone to the gallows in his place.

poor and inexperienced driver; why would an experienced car thief like James Hanratty need to be shown the gears of a car as unsophisticated as a Morris Minor if he, indeed, was the driver that night?

In 1963, after Alphon confessed to the killing in tape recordings, Justice submitted a long memorandum to the Home Office. Part of the recording goes: 'I was there to separate a couple of people in a car. That was the motive. That is why it took five hours. Five f***ing hours it took. You've got your motive.' He said he had been paid £5,000 for his night's work. Alphon said he

Above: *Det Constable Bert Stillings, left, and Det-Con Jim Williams, who arrested Hanratty for murder.*

was a hired gun, paid for by a man he did not want to name, to separate Michael Gregsten from Miss Storie so he would return to his wife. He claimed that he wanted to frighten Gregsten and attack her, but that it had all gone terribly wrong when Gregsten attacked him with the laundry bag. In July 1963 the matter was formally raised in Parliament by Fenner Brockway MP, who argued for Hanratty's innocence and backed his arguments by reading from the transcripts of the tapes. The Home Office was unmoved; Hanratty was guilty as far as they were concerned and that was that.

Paul Foot, the distinguished campaigning journalist, remains convinced of Hanratty's innocence after many years of probing the affair. He said: 'I made contact with Alphon and then began a three-year ordeal of late-night phone calls in which Alphon taunted me with his confessions. I met him for the first time face-to-face 1969. On a cold November afternoon we walked from Brighton to Hove and back, talking all the time. He was spruce and polite – although on the phone he could work himself up to terrible furies – and he talked in riddles, contradicting himself and constantly shifting the details of his story. But in all our meetings he never deviated from his admission that he committed the murder.

'Between 1966 and 1971 I went again to Rhyl. I interviewed fourteen witnesses who supported in varying degrees of certainty Hanratty's story about his two nights there in August 1961. It is impossible, in my view, to read the testimony of these people and not to believe that Hanratty was wan-

Above: Hanratty's father outside Parliament handing leaflets to passers-by. He marched on Downing Street, below, with supportors to petition against the death sentence passed on his son.

dering the streets of Rhyl looking for lodgings at the very moment the gunman was climbing into Gregsten's Morris Minor some two hundred and fifty miles away.' Foot also claims that Alphon produced proof that he had been paid £5,000, a substantial sum of money in those days.

A DETERMINED CONFESSION

The case did not end there. In 1967 Alphon, who was facing prosecution over harassment of people involved in the case, went to the Hotel du Louvre in Paris where he called a press conference on the case. He announced openly that he was the A6 murderer and later he wrote to Roy Jenkins, Home Secretary, saying he would be willing to confess to him in person. Nothing was done. In 1971, one hundred MPs signed a motion calling for a public inquiry into the case. Jenkins had been succeeded by this time by Reginald Maudling, who also refused to act. In 1974 the newly-elected Labour government commissioned

Left: *James Hanratty Snr with two other sons, Peter and Michael, arrive at court on the day his son, James, was to be sentenced.*

Below: *Mr and Mrs Hanratty have always believed in the innocence of their son. His death for a murder he swore he never committed was a bitter tragedy for the family.*

a secret report on the case from barrister Lewis Hawser – Hawser pronounced Hanratty Guilty. The government was convinced that it was time once and for all to shut the lid on the Hanratty case.

However, in 1992, film-maker Bob Woffinden tracked down Alphon, now in his sixties and living in Kings Cross, London. He still admits to the murder.

In a written statement to former barrister Jeremy Fox said: 'The crime was a result of a conspiracy that had its roots in the infidelity of Michael Gregsten with Valerie Storie. I was offered money to terrorise the couple and a criminal, Charlie 'Dixie' France provided the gun. What I thought I might do was terrorise the pair for a while, then lock Gregsten in the boot while I had some preliminary fun with the girl. I would later take him out of the boot, tie him up in the cornfield and depart with the girl.' The old man, Alphon, referred to himself in the statement as 'I, the killer'.

Right: *Police control the long queue of people trying to enter the court for Hanratty's trial.*

Below: *Mr Michael Sherrard on the right was defence counsel for Hanratty.*

Woffinden's documentary screened on Britain's Channel Four network also cast reasonable doubt on Valerie Storie's identification of Hanratty as the guilty man. The film showed that in a statement to police at the time Miss Storie had doubts before the identification of Hanratty about her ability to recognise the killer. 'My memory of this man's face is fading,' she said. 'I am so afraid that when I am confronted with the man I may not be able to pick him out.' This crucial statement was not made available to the jury at Hanratty's trial.

When Woffinden's film was broadcast, campaigners again approached the Home Office seeking a new inquiry while asking for DNA samples from Scotland Yard evidence files. If the samples were made available, a DNA match using the DNA profile of his surviving relatives could be made that might clear Hanratty. The samples of the murderer's DNA survive on clothing worn by Miss Storie on the night of the crime. Geoffrey Birdman, solicitor

Below, left: Valerie Storie arrives in an ambulance to bear witness against Hanratty. She identified him as the man who killed her lover before raping and attacking her.

Below: Mr Justice Gorman who, in accordance with the law, passed the death sentence on Hanratty when the jury returned a Guilty verdict.

for the Hanratty family, said: 'There is now overwhelming evidence to indicate that Hanratty had nothing whatsoever to do with this crime and was totally innocent.' The Home Office has agreed tentatively to look at any new evidence but has so far not agreed to a full-blown inquiry. Neither has Scotland Yard yet agreed to hand over the DNA samples or the sixteen boxes of papers collected by London detectives who led the investigation. Journalist Paul Foot who still retains an abiding interest in the case has said: 'James Hanratty cannot walk free. His will probably not be the last miscarriage of justice, but it is likely to remain one of the most shameful.'

MATA HARI
Woman of Mystery

Was Mata Hari really a spy or just the ultimate good-time girl who couldn't resist a man in a uniform? This femme fatale never made a secret of taking lovers for money but denied charges of spying. The evidence suggests that a court today would agree with her plea of innocence.

She has gone down in legend as the supreme seductress, the spy whose military lovers betrayed their nations in pillow talk. Sultry, sexy, shrouded in mystery, Mata Hari – her adopted Javanese name means 'eye of the day' – moved in the highest circles before and during First World War. However, in 1917 her sex life led her to be classified as a German spy. On 15 October, as a wintry autumn sun was just rising, she was executed by a French firing squad. Later, the beautiful body that was admired from a distance by Parisian audiences who watched her dance, and from closer range by numerous officers of both Germany and France, was dissected in medical experiments by trainee doctors.

But was she a spy? Mata Hari – real name Margaretha Gertruida Zelle – was executed at a time when the nations of Europe were gripped in a communal madness that threatened to blight Western civilisation for ever. As men died by the million in places like Chemin-des-Dames, Verdun, the Somme, Passchaendale, Vimy Ridge and Champagne, governments needed to make their sacrifices appear worthy and to prevent further bloodletting.

Spy fever was rife in the capitals of Europe. Intelligence agencies looked for spies everywhere and, if they found them, the accused paid the ultimate penalty. In wartime there is little time for balanced inquiry when the fate of a nation might depend on the secrecy of a single piece of information. But, with hindsight, it seems likely that Mata Hari died for her sexuality as much as for any state secrets – real or imagined – that she may have passed on to her alleged spymasters.

From Dutch peasant girl to a woman of beauty and intrigue was a long journey for Margaretha, born in the tiny hamlet of Leeuwarden in Holland on 7 August 1876. Her mother came from a prominent Dutch family, her father, Adam, was a business-

Opposite: *A dazzling pose from the good-time girl who was to be executed when she was accused of being most famous female spy in the world, Mata Hari.*

Below: *Mata Hari, the belly dancer, entranced her male audiences.*

man. Her life was settled and eminently respectable until 1891 when her mother died and her father, stricken with grief, sold up in Leeuwarden and moved to Amsterdam to try his luck there. With him went Margaretha and her three younger brothers. By this time she had blossomed early into a Lolita-type beauty, advanced for her age, with an interest in men that her father felt bordered on the unhealthy. Indeed, she had to be removed from one school, where she tried to seduce the director, and was sent to live with an uncle in The Hague, who, her father and teachers hoped, would teach her some discipline.

In 1895 she answered an advertisement in a daily newspaper placed by Captain Rudolf MacLeod, a Dutch officer of Scots descent, who was seeking a wife after long overseas service in the Dutch East Indies colonies. Margaretha, who by this time had shown herself a woman whose heart beat faster for men in uniform, met the dashing Captain MacLeod after sending him a picture of herself. Within ten days they were lovers and two months later – with Margaretha pregnant – they married at Amsterdam town hall.

If Captain MacLeod was captivated by her voluptuous beauty, he was by no means so keen on her penchant for the good life. He hoped that with the birth of their son Norman on 30 January 1896, she might become more restrained in her spending habits but he was to be disappointed.

A LOST CHILD, A LOST MARRIAGE

The following year Captain MacLeod was promoted to Major and was re-posted to Indonesia, this time taking along with him his spendthrift wife. In 1898 she gave birth to a second child, a daughter named Juana Luisa, but by this time the marriage was almost on the rocks. Major MacLeod was unhappy with rumours of his wife's behaviour with junior officers. He took to drinking heavily and reportedly threatened her with his service revolver and even beat her with a whip. In 1899 he was transferred to Sumatra and his wife delayed following him for two months. When she did arrive her son Norman looked so ill that a doctor was called. The boy hovered on the brink of death for a fortnight before he died, poisoned by a bitter servant girl who thought she had suffered some slight at Margaretha's hands. The boy's death hastened the end of the marriage. In 1902, when MacLeod retired and was living back in Holland with Margaretha, she finally plucked up the courage to divorce him.

The modest allowance given to her by her ex-husband was quite inadequate for a woman with the tastes of Margaretha. After considering a career on the stage – she decided against it because she thought she would have to train for too long – she settled on becoming a dancer and moved to Paris in 1903. Supplementing her meagre allowance by working as an artist's model

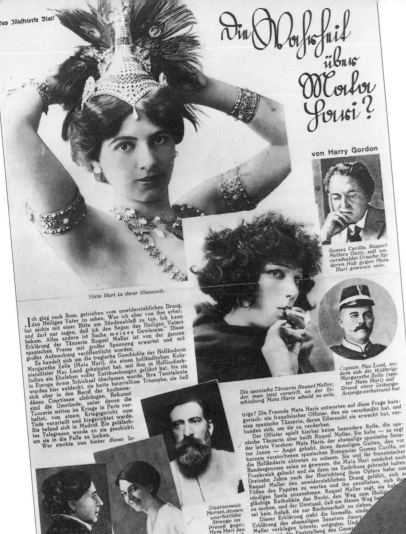

Die Wahrheit über Mata Hari?

von Harry Gordon

Mata Hari in ihrer Glanzzeit.

Ich ging nach Rom, getrieben vom unwiderstehlichen Drang, den Heiligen Vater zu sehen. Was ich aber von ihm erbat, hat nichts mit einer Bitte um Sündenablaß zu tun. Ich kann und darf nur sagen, daß ich den Segen des Heiligen Vaters bekam. Alles andere ist Sache meines Gewissens. Diese Erklärung der Tänzerin Raquel Meller ist von der ganzen spanischen Presse mit großer Spannung erwartet worden.

Es handelt sich um die tragische Geschichte der Holländerin Margarethe Zelle (Mata Hari), die einen holländischen Kolonialoffizier Mac Leod geheiratet hat, mit ihm in Holländisch-Indien ein Eheleben voller Enttäuschungen geführt hat, his sie in Europa ihrem Schicksal überlassen wurde. Ihre Tanztalente wurden hier entdeckt, sie hatte beispiellose Triumphe, sie ließ sich aber in den Beruf der hochmondänen Courtisane abdrängen. Bekannt sind die Umstände, unter denen sie als Tänzerin mitten im Kriege in Paris verhaftet, von einem Kriegsgericht zum Tode verurteilt und hingerichtet wurde. Sie befand sich in Madrid. Ein gefälschtes Telegramm wurde an sie geschickt, um sie in die Falle zu locken. Wer steckte nun hinter dieser In-

Gomez Carillo, Raquel Mellers Gatte, soll unverschuldet Ursache für deren Haß gegen Mata Hari gewesen sein.

Die spanische Tänzerin Raquel Meller, der man jetzt vorwirft, an der Erschiebung Mata Haris schuld zu sein.

Captain Mac Leod, mit dem sich die 16jährige Margarethe Zelle (später Mata Hari) auf Grund einer Zeitungs-Anzeige verheiratet hat

trige? Die Freunde Mata Haris antworten auf diese Frage kategorisch: ein französischer Offizier, den sie verschmäht hat, und eine spanische Tänzerin, deren Eifersucht sie erweckt hat, verbanden sich, um sie zu verderben.

Der Offizier spielt hierbei keine besondere Rolle, die spanische Tänzerin aber heißt Raquel Meller. Sie habe — so sagt der letzte Verehrer Mata Haris, der ehemalige spanische Senator Junoy — Angst gehabt, ihren damaligen Gatten, den vor kurzem verstorbenen spanischen Romancier Gomez Carillo, an die Holländerin abtreten zu müssen. Sie und ihr französischer Bundesgenosse seien es gewesen, die Mata Hari zunächst nach Frankreich gelockt und sie dann ins Zuchthaus gebracht haben. Dreizehn Jahre nach der Hinrichtung ihres Opfers habe nun Raquel Meller den unwiderstehlichen Drang gefühlt, sich zu Füßen des Papstes zu werfen und ihn anzuflehen, sich ihrer sündigen Seele anzunehmen. Raquel Meller sagt, sie hab... gläubige Katholikin das Recht, den Weg zum Heilig... zu suchen, und der Umstand, daß sie diesen Weg beb... sei kein Anlaß, sie zur Rechenschaft zu ziehen.

Dieser Erklärung steht die formelle, einde... Erklärung des ehemaligen Senators Junoy... Meller verklagen könnte, entgegen. Und... trifft, so ist die Feststellung des Gene... der ehemaligen deutschen Spionsgie... Listen des deutschen Spionagedien... nicht aus der Welt zu schaffen.

Warum mußte Mata Hari als... werden? Kriegspsychose? Mac...

Staatsanwalt Mornet, dessen unerbittliche Strenge im Prozeß gegen Mata Hari den Ausschlag gab.

Mata Hari als Insassin des Frauenzuchthauses Saint-Lazare, von wo aus sie zur Hinrichtung geführt wurde.

Louise-Jeanne Mac Leod, die im Jahre 1919 gestorbene einzige Tochter Mata Haris.

expossed, tanned flesh. In Monte Carlo, Paris and later Vienna, her exotic 'Hindu dances' were the talk of Europe and the hazy details of her background only served to make her that much more appealing.

During this time, Mata Hari began to indulge herself in more affairs of the heart and she flitted with ease between the bedrooms of German, French and Dutch officers. By the end of 1914, when Europe was at war, she was in Berlin and had taken the capital's chief of police, a Herr von Jagow, as one of her lovers, for which she was paid the princely sum of £1,500 per year. At her trial she would later deny that she was a prostitute, saying of the financial reward: 'It was merely what I was worth!'

Mata Hari journeyed back to Paris in 1916 after visiting her homeland. She was now at the centre of the attention of French counter-espionage agents who knew of her

as she sought employment as a dancer in the French capital, Margaretha became a much sought-after nude model for numerous Parisian artists. She did not want to strip but decided she had to 'for the sake of my daughter'. There are unsubstantiated stories that she also became a prostitute in a high-class brothel but no firm proof of this activity has ever surfaced.

She tried to capitalise on her stay in the East by becoming something of a woman of mystery in her dances. She dyed her skin an exotic bronze colour and dressed in flowing, oriental-style robes and veils. She adopted the name Mata Hari and soon gained a reputation in Paris that went wildly beyond the bounds of truth. Mata Hari was keen to play up the idea that she was a woman from India, a high-born aristocrat who danced to forget her broken heart. Reviews of her dances were usually pretty scathing but all critics concurred that she was, at least, pleasing to look at, her costumes revealing daring glimpses of highly-placed German lovers (she had more than one in Berlin) and who believed she was on a mission to spy for them. Apparently one of the pieces of evidence which brought her to their attention came from the Italian secret service who reported that the previous year she had been aboard a Japanese vessel docked at Naples, Italy, a French and British ally in the First World War, reported: 'While examining the passenger list we have recognised the name of a theatrical celebrity called Mata Hari. She has it seems renounced her claims to Indian birth and become Berlinoise. She speaks German with a slight eastern accent.'

The French were also tipped off by British secret service agents who said that she had been seen on several occasions in the company of German officers in Madrid, Spain, then a neutral country and a hotbed of espionage during the war. She actually landed in England on one trip and was taken to Scotland Yard where she was accused of spying – which she denied – before being taken back to Portsmouth and put on a ship bound again for Spain.

Right: *Captain McLeod divorced his flighty wife. The stipend he gave her afterwards gave her was not enough for her expensive tastes so she went to work as Mata Hari, a 'woman of mystery'.*

Mata Hari was under the watchful eyes of officers of the Deuxième Bureau of counter-intelligence, when she travelled back to France and visited an injured Captain Marov, a Russian who had been wounded while fighting for France. They took her visit to be a smokescreen for spying on Allied airfields near Vittel and claimed later at her trial that she was gathering intelligence on the order of battle of French forces at Verdun – the worst battle of the war that eventually claimed more than eight hundred thousand French lives. More information about monies she had received from highly-placed German officers was passed from French agents in Berlin and, towards the end of 1916, Mata Hari was arrested in her hotel suite near Vittel and charged with high treason; her hearing was to be held in secret before a military court martial that was closed to both the public and press.

She was charged with seven cases of espionage. They were: that in 1916 she dealt in intelligence matters with the enemy in Spain; that in 1915 she had dealt in intelligence matters with the enemy in Holland; that in 1916 she had dealt in intelligence matters with the enemy in France; that she passed military information to German agents in Spain; that she entered the 'entrenched camp of Paris to procure information to the enemy's profit'; that she informed the enemy of a coming French offensive; that she warned the enemy of the discovery of a new chemical ink.

However, at the trial it became evident that French evidence was scanty, based more on their own fears and prejudices about her than on any solid evidence. It was based on bank receipts from her German lovers, her relationship with Herr von Jagow and a French mistrust of a woman who crossed borders with utter fearlessness during wartime. There was also more than a hint that French *savoir-faire* did not extend to her lovers in the German military. Here she is being cross-examined about Herr von Jagow:

Prosecution: But he enlisted you in the German secret service.

Mata Hari: No.

Prosecution: Do you deny that you were known as H.21?

Mata Hari: No.

Prosecution: That was your code number in the German secret service?

Above: *Mata Hari was a sensation in Monte Carlo, Paris and Berlin. Her alluring costumes were scandalous in an age when women were modest in their dress.*

THERE WAS MORE THAN A HINT THAT FRENCH SAVOIRE-FAIRE DID NOT EXTEND TO HER LOVERS IN THE GERMAN MILITARY.

Left: *The bell at St Lazare prison tolled her death after she faced a firing squad.*

Below: *Mata Hari dressed in furs shortly before her execution.*

made repeated calls to the German consulate at Vigo. Without hesitation Mata Hari said: 'Of course, they were my lovers of the moment!' As were, she said, Major von Specht, chief of German espionage in Amsterdam and another officer who was based in the Hague.

The French produced evidence of a telegraph cipher from Madrid about a payment of Fr15,000 made to her through a diplomatic pouch to Holland. This inordinately large sum was, they said, payment for passing on information to the Germans of a French offensive planned for the Champagne area. 'No,' cried Mata Hari. 'I... I tell you, it was to pay for my nights of love. That is my price. Believe me, be gallant, gentlemen – French officers!'

Her advocate did his best for her; a highly-placed diplomat in the French Foreign Office was called to testify on her behalf. The man, who has not been named in all

Mata Hari: Oh no. My lover gave me the sign so that he could correspond with me. He could use official methods if ordinary ones failed in wartime. Further, he could use official money to pay me.

Prosecution: You were in Berlin well away from the war. Then via Belgium, Holland and England you came to France. In wartime – why?

Mata Hari: I wished to dispose of my property at Neuilly.

Prosecution: But that only needed a few weeks and yet you stayed for seven months.

Mata Hari: I went to Vittel, to be near Captain Marov, the only man I ever loved. He was blind – I wished to consecrate my life to his welfare.

Prosecution: But while at Vittel you met many officers?

Mata Hari: Doubtless. There were officers everywhere. I like officers!

It was soon apparent to the French prosecuting team that she was exceedingly willing to be branded a harlot or a scarlet woman – but never a traitor. There was plenty of circumstantial evidence that suggested she was certainly one and possibly both. Captain Georges Ledoux testified that he had seen her in Madrid with a Major Kalle, the German military attache attached to the embassy there, Lieutenant von Krohn, the naval attaché and that she had

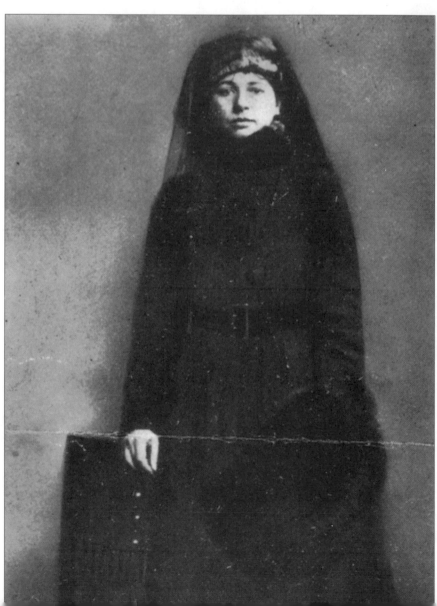

these years, told the court that in his 'long and intimate' acquaintance with her he had never known her to be anything other than a courtesan. Certainly she had never enquired of military secrets from him – and he knew plenty, after all.

Some of the French suppositions about Mata Hari's spying activities are so far fetched as to border on utter preposterousness. For instance, she was accused, while at Vittel, of spying out French arrangements for an attack on the Chemin-des-Dames in Champagne. How? It is one hundred and thirty miles from the scene of the planned attack (an attack, incidentally, which was a monumental failure like most of the offensives planned by the General Staff during the war). More importantly – the attack was actually over before she even went to Vittel. They accused her of reporting the French mutinies that swept through the ranks at Verdun, that threatened to break the backbone of the army and, consequently, the will of France to resist. The Germans did not learn about these mutinies until after the Armistice.

She was also accused of leaking naval secrets to her German naval attaché lover – specifically that she passed on secrets of French troopships and merchant supply vessels for enemy U-boats to sink. She did not know a single code or military cipher and post-war German naval intelligence records show that Mata Hari provided no information at all to the Kriegsmarine during its active operations.

A SUPERLATIVE FEMALE SPY

Furthermore, after the war, the Germans never acknowledged that Mata Hari – branded in the closing speeches of the court martial as 'the most dangerous and damaging female spy in the history of the world' – worked for them in any capacity at all. No file in German intelligence history has ever been unearthed that suggested she passed on anything more to her consorts than what was in the daily newspapers in the European capitals. The whole affair smacked of a witch hunt and her arrest drew protests from some of the most prominent people in Europe. The Crown Prince of Germany, son of the Kaiser, and the Prime Minister of Holland, Dutch statesman Mynheer van den Linden and the

Prince Consort of the Netherlands were among the dignitaries who voiced their opposition to her trial.

Nevertheless, she was found Guilty and duly sentenced to be executed by firing squad. After two days in a padded cell, where she was watched to see if she would try to commit suicide, Mata Hari was taken to cell twelve on death row at St Lazare jail, Vincennes. She read a Buddhist book of faith while she sat in the cell waiting for the sentence to be carried out – she claimed she had renounced all ties to any Western faith – and danced her oriental dances in attempts to forget her impending doom. One of her former lovers, a young Frenchman, planned to spring her from the jail in a dramatic and romantic gesture that came to nothing. Her execution was fixed for Monday 15 October. Dr Bizard, a police surgeon, called on her the evening before the court's sentence was to be carried out and gave her a strong sleeping draught.

Above: *Mata Hari in street clothes. She maintained that she was not interested in espionage, but she did like men in uniforms.*

'THE MOST DANGEROUS AND DAMAGING FEMALE SPY IN THE HISTORY OF THE WORLD.'

Below: *In wartime, it is usual to despatch traitors swiftly by putting them before a firing squad. This was to be Mata Hari's fate, although this is a photograph of another's execution.*

The following morning, as she was led to her place of execution in the dried up moat of the Château of Vincennes, she gaily asked a guard if she might put on a little lace corset. He agreed she could. She also put on a bright hat, but was puzzled that she could not have a pin for it; she was told pins were forbidden to prisoners in case they tried to do themselves harm.

about to kill her she said mockingly: 'What is the purpose of executing at dawn? In India it is not so; there death is a penalty that is made into a ceremony – in full daylight before crowds of guests and to the sweet scent of jasmine. I would have preferred to lunch with friends and then gone to Vincennes in the afternoon. But you choose to shoot me on an empty stomach. It is so unreasonable.'

Mata Hari was tied at the wrists to the execution post but refused the blindfold always offered to the condemned. Twelve soldiers were given the command to fire. In the split second before twelve bullets pounded into her a faint smile played across her lips. A sergeant advanced moments later to administer the *coup de grace* with his pistol in the back of her head and a doctor later testified that she had breathed her last; at least one bullet had penetrated clean through her lace corset into her heart. The beautiful, much-loved body was later cut up for use by medical students.

'REASONABLE DOUBT'

Since her death the name Mata Hari has passed into legend and everyday usage. Whenever a female agent is caught or written about she instantly becomes 'the most famous spy since Mata Hari'. A woman with wiles and a feminine attraction dangerous to men is branded a Mata Hari. Those with many lovers, too, are branded with the name of the woman who died in that dusty old moat of a French château. But it is almost certain that she was not a spy – and probably, had she been tried today, her behaviour would have been questionable but the evidence would have been poor enough for 'reasonable doubt' to acquit her. A study of her trial shows at least four salient miscarriages of justice.

First, hearsay evidence was submitted that would under no circumstances be allowed in any court – military or civil – today. No proof was advanced save she received Fr15,000. The French insisted this and other payments were for her espionage activies, while she, a beautiful courtesan, maintained it was for sexual favours. Incidentally, there were plenty of precedents for the reference of the French authorities about military officials paying their mistresses out of official funds.

AS SHE WAS LED TO HER EXECUTION SHE ASKED A GUARD IF SHE MAY WEAR A LITTLE CORSET... AND A BRIGHT HAT.

Mata Hari showed bravery and gallantry in the face of death. Before she was led away she gave to Sister Leonide, a nun who was in attendance, a bunch of letters to be posted after the execution to numerous old flames and friends. 'Don't get the addresses mixed up,' she said, 'otherwise you will cause distress and upset to many, many families.' As the gentle nun began to cry, the condemned woman said: 'Since I must die, I must be resigned. I leave for the big station from which there is no return ticket. Now little mother, don't cry... how little you are. It would take two of you to make a Mata Hari.'

As she turned to the officer in charge of the firing party she said: 'I am ready, you may kill me.' When he, in turn, asked if she had any last statements to make, she replied: 'Yes. You may write that Mata Hari declares she is innocent and a victim of murder.' Scoffing at the men who were

Second, the prosecution was unable to prove that she engaged in espionage when she came to Vittel.

Third, all the men questioned at her trial – her lovers and her confidantes – who had access to classified military information, swore that they never passed on any intelligence or state secrets. If that were the case, then what could she have passed on to her German contacts save that which was already in the public domain?

Fourth, the French alleged she was paid over the years a total of Fr75,000 for spying but they could not offer proof to counter Mata Hari's claim that this was merely income from her lovers.

In 1985 an American journalist, Russell Warren Howe, claimed that he was shown secret papers relating to the trial at Vincennes, the very place of her death. He claimed that the intelligence he received showed that she was not a German spy but a freelance operative whose sole espionage effort was in Madrid where she actually worked for the French. Howe says she seduced a German intelligence agent there, meaning to pass on the secrets he told her to the French, possibly in return for money.

Howe maintains she did give the Germans who became her lovers information on the French war effort – but she used stories that were culled from newspapers and street gossip. She was never in a position to jeapardise whole offensives, nor learn the secrets of chemical ink, as was ludicrously stated at her trial. But the French in 1916, having suffered appalling losses throughout the war and major mutinies in their ranks at Verdun which literally threatened to smash the national will to fight on, were looking for a scapegoat. It is fair to comment that it was easier to blame a treacherous woman spy than incompetent generals.

If she was a spy, then she broke every cardinal rule ever laid down for practitioners of that sly, dark world. She was high profile, remained high profile, never met with her contacts in any places other than top European hotels or at magnificent country estates. Historians who have studied her case over the years think it inconceivable that she had the political skill or motive to have contributed to the deaths of hundreds of thousands of allied servicemen, as was alleged at her trial.

In the Fifties, one historian wrote of her: 'Mata Hari was not a sympathetic character; there can be no question of presenting her as a romantic heroine. But a courtesan – even a spy – is entitled to justice. The atmosphere of the hour must be taken into account. The influence of defeat and mutiny must have militated against impartial judgement for Mata Hari appeared as one of the reasons for the current distress. No court is infallible. It may be that the French have more definite proofs of the woman's guilt than they have ever made known, or that were produced at the trial. If so they should be revealed. There can be nothing secret about them after such a lapse of time. If not, there is a case for the complete re-examination of the Mata Hari affair.' He wrote further observations about the case. 'She was no Joan of Arc, but her claim to justice is just as strong. The French need have no fears. It is not a sign of weakness but of strength to admit that you may have been wrong. Until a formal re-assessment is made possible, I imagine that many people will favour the old Scottish verdict of "not proven".'

> IT MAY BE THAT THE FRENCH HAVE MORE DEFINITE PROOF OF THE WOMAN'S GUILT THAN THEY HAVE EVER MADE KNOWN.

Below: *Many accused spies were summarily shot during the Great War. They were put against a cross as they faced the bullets. Mata Hari showed great courage in the face of death, and wore a cheeky corset and pretty hat for her execution.*

STEFAN KISZKO
A Malicious Prank

How does a gentle tax clerk get locked away as a brutal sex-murderer in modern Britain? Stefan Kiszko spent sixteen years in prison as a result of a malicious prank. The system that is meant to protect ordinary citizens failed with frightening ease.

Prison, with all its punishments, menace and stigma, is bad enough at the best of times. To live within its walls as a rapist or, worse, a child molestor, is hard indeed; yet this was what simple-minded Stefan Kiszko endured for sixteen years. For he was trapped in a nightmare of Kafkaesque proportions; an innocent man in jail for the brutal sex killing of an eleven-year-old girl.

Finally, from the shadows of this monstrous injustice, Stefan emerged blinking into the sunlight of freedom in February 1992. Waiting for him, as she had waited every day was his mother, the courageous-woman who believed he was innocent and who took on the full majesty and weight of British law to prove it.

Charlotte Kiszko was fifty when police called on her modest home in Rochdale in 1975 to say that her son Stefan was wanted for questioning in connection with the murder of eleven-year-old Lesley Molseed. Little Lesley was found on a lonely Yorkshire moor in October 1975. She had been abducted while out shopping on an errand for her mother and her violated body found on moorland near to Rochdale. She had been dragged from a car, stabbed and sexually assaulted. Her clothes were stained with semen and these stains would prove vital both in Stefan's conviction and later to prove his innocence. These moors were notoious because Hindley and Brady buried their child victims there.

'My first thought,' said Charlotte in a voice strongly accented by the gutteral tones of her own native Slovenian language, 'was that the police only want to talk to Stefan. They asked him to go to the police station and he drove there in his own car. He never came back.

'When I begged them to let me speak to him or to just give him a message that I was all right, they refused me even that. I didn't think you could get solicitors on a Sunday, but then I wasn't prepared for that, we have never been in any kind of trouble before. You don't know what to do for the best when it comes along.' It was 21 December 1975.

Stefan, a tax clerk, was regarded in his town as a kind of gentle-but-dim bachelor; overweight, an obvious introvert who was clumsy with girls. His life seemed to revolve in turns around his mother, his Hillman car which she had bought for him and his job. He was neither a drinker nor a gambler, and had a limited social life.

HORMONAL MEDICATION

The first time he had come to the attention of the police was just weeks before Lesley's body was found. Local girls in Rochdale trooped into a police station to report Stefan for exposing himself to them. Much later they admitted that they had made the allegation up 'for a lark'. They thought Stefan 'stupid' and all had a good laugh at his discomfort at the thought of the police interviewing him.

The police interviewed him three times and discovered two things about him: that he was infertile and that he was taking hormonal medication to ease his condition. One of these crucial factors remained hidden at his later trial for the murder of Lesley Molseed.

Around the time of the killing Stefan was receiving injections of the male hormone testosterone to combat his medical condition of hypogonadism, the root cause of his infertility. The drug was meant to increase his sperm count and thereby his sexual drive. Four samples of semen found on Lesley's battered body were analysed at a forensic laboratory in Harrogate, Yorkshire, by Peter Guise, a specialist forensic scientist working for Ron Outteridge, a distinguished forensic expert

HIS LIFE SEEMED TO REVOLVE IN TURNS AROUND HIS MOTHER, HIS HILLMAN CAR WHICH SHE HAD BOUGHT FOR HIM AND HIS JOB.

for the police in Yorkshire who had handled literally thousands of cases.

Guise found that the semen on Lesley's clothing contained 'sperm-heads', medical proof that her killer was a fertile man. Further examination revealed that the sperm count was, however, perculiarly low, in the bottom twenty-five per cent of sperm density. Armed with this information the police officers in charge of the case – tough Yorkshire coppers Detective Chief Superintendent Jack Dibb and Detective Superintendent Dick Holland – went in search of Stefan Kiszko.

For two days Stefan, the simple-minded tax clerk was subjected to intense interrogation. He was not allowed access to a

Below: *Stefan Kiszko with his loving mother, Charlotte in the happy days before he was wrongfully arrested for the murder of a little girl.*

solicitor and was unable to successfully give himself an alibi for the time of the murder. Mrs Kiszko said later: 'They [the police] regarded Stefan as some kind of village-idiot. I think they had already made up their minds about him before he was even in the police station.'

On the second day of Stefan's confinement in custody he signed a detailed confession to the murder that, sixteen years later, would be proved to be totally forced and false. Stefan would tell how the statement was in fact written by a police officer and that he signed it 'because I was scared'. He was a timid man of low intelligence.

The statement was enough to secure his conviction.

His trial in July 1976 was a farce of circumstantial evidence, forensic tests on some fibres found on Lesley's clothes and Stefan's own confession. The fibres had supposedly come from a carpet square in Stefan's home – a carpet that was one of the top-selling brands in the north of England and probably was in thousands of homes. The fibre evidence was used as damning testimony.

RE-INVESTIGATION OF THE CASE

Dr Edward Tierney, a police surgeon, carried out a test on Kiszko and found him to be suffering from hypogonadism. Tierney said: 'My physical examination confirmed that he indeed suffered from this affliction. I did not know of the discrepancy between Kiszko's and the killer's semen until after the Home Office ordered a re-investigation of the whole affair.'

What happened, in fact, was that the tests taken by Guise were not mentioned during the trial and Stefan Kiszko was framed. Outteridge, Guise's boss, submitted a statement to the trial referring to the semen stains on the girl's body, but did not mention the discrepancy between the sperm-heads found there by his junior and Stefan's inability, backed up by Dr Tierney, to produce sperm.

His solicitor was David Waddington, QC, now Lord Privy Seal and leader of the House of Lords. He advised his client to run a defence of 'diminished responsibility' on medical grounds and claimed that the testosterone injections he was receiving had boosted his sex drive in

Above: *The murdered child's family wept when they learned that the wrong man had been imprisoned for the crime. Her sister, Julie Crabb is supported by her father, Fred Anderson on the left, and her brother, Fred Anderson Jnr.*

some uncontrollable way. By a 10-2 majority verdict Stefan Kiszko, condemned for a crime he never committed, was consigned to the miserable prison life of a sex offender.

In Wakefield prison he was put on Rule 43, the segregation policy practised in jails to keep sex offenders safe from vengeance. Year after year his mental condition deteriorated until he was diagnosed as an acute schizophrenic. Meanwhile, his mother was battling for him in a fight that seemed hopeless but would one day lead to victory.

Charlotte, a widow, always refused to accept the verdict and knew in her heart of hearts that her son was no sex killer. She says: 'I knew he hadn't done it. When you see a child grow up and you are very close to them you can spot the changes in them. I know my son was having a course of testosterone injections around the time of the murder and a lot of people liked to say they turned him into a monster, but that was all just rubbish.

'The first solicitor I went to wouldn't help. He didn't bother about witnesses or evidence. My sister and I went to him and told him that the poor girl had eleven stab wounds on her body. So why didn't they find blood on my son's clothes or body or in his car? And he said to me that all the blood went inside the girl's body. I told him that I had grown up on a farm and that when you kill a chicken there is blood. He called me a hysterical woman and assured me that there was nothing to be done. I always remember his words: "That is the law of this country and that is the end of it."

'But I knew he hadn't done it. On Saturdays and Sundays my son never left me alone for longer than half an hour and the Sunday of the murder was no different. We went to the cemetary together to put flowers on my husband's grave. I remember very well coming home because there was a fire in the street – then Stefan took the car to the car wash and went to see if his aunt Freda needed anything. They didn't think a mother knew if her son had just popped off and turned into a murderer in ten minutes? I knew he hadn't. '

'THEY DIDN'T THINK A MOTHER KNEW IF HER SON HAD JUST POPPED OFF AND TURNED INTO A MURDERER IN TEN MINUTES?'

She had neither the money nor the public support to bring pressure for a re-investigation of the case. But five years ago, with her solicitor Campbell Malone, and a dogged private eye called Peter Jackson, she took on the establishment to save her son from his living hell.

Jackson, a former RAF policeman, turned up the clues which finally led to the shameful miscarriage of justice being exposed. Jackson thought of the case initially as a routine investigation but 'I became alarmed as I looked further into the case. In my view the police and the defence were both at fault. I wanted it all to come out so that no other poor devil could ever fall into the same trap.'

When he began investigating nobody knew about the forensic evidence on the semen samples, long forgotten in police files. Jackson discovered that Stefan remembered being in a corner shop on the Sunday of the murder and he heard a row between customers. Jackson did establish from other witnesses that the row had taken place and that Stefan had been present.

FOUR WITNESSES SAW A RED CAR, STEFAN'S CAR WAS BRONZE

Jackson also sought to destroy the credibility of Stefan's 'confession'. A witness said she had seen Lesley Molseed on the day of the murder in a white car with red markings around the wings. Three other witnesses had also reported seeing a similar car near to the murder scene. Stefan's Hillman car was bronze coloured.

All this evidence was sent in a file to the Home Secretary who ordered an internal inquiry of the West Yorkshire police force. That inquiry turned up the 'missing' slides with the semen samples that could have proved Stefan Kiszko innocent all those years ago. They proved it now. Three appeal court judges ruled in February 1992 that he was a wrongly convicted man. Quashing the conviction Lord Lane, the Lord Chief Justice, said: 'The result is that this man cannot have been the person responsible for the ejaculation and, consequently, cannot have been the murderer.'

Stefan was forty when he walked free from jail with the lost years behind him. He was a broken man in many ways, suffering from chronic schizophrenia brought on by his imprisonment. He said: 'My years inside were a hell and a nightmare, but I never lost faith that I would be acquitted. I always believed the courts would come on my side. But I always believed in my own innocence.' Smiling broadly, he turned to his mother, kissed her, and said: 'Mum has given me every confidence. What would I have done without her?'

So what went wrong with British justice? An inquiry has been ordered by the Home Office into why the scientific evidence wasn't available at the trial and its outcome is still a considerable way off. The people involved now hold some of the highest positions in the land but will still have to account to the Lancashire police carrying out the inquiy. Peter Taylor, the barrister who led the prosecution of Stefan – and who is now the Lord Chief Justice – will be asked if he knew why the key evidence regarding Stefan was not produced at his trial. The same will be asked of Lord Waddington and Dick Holland, who now works as a security expert. Chief Superintendent Kenneth Mackay, who is heading the inquiry, said: 'I will need to talk to a lot of people. They will all be interviewed in time.'

Campbell Malone believes it is 'most unlikely' that the evidence of a semen mismatch was contained in the bundle of papers handed to Taylor and Waddington as they prepared for Kiszko's trial. He says he has seen most of the papers made available to the lawyers involved in the case and claims that there is only one paragraph which mentions semen, saying it was impossible to identify the attacker's blood group by testing the sperm found on the girl's body. Dick Holland has made a statement saying that he did not see written documents suggesting samples from Kiszko and from the body were incompatible. He added that, at the time of the arrest, he was not informed, that there was a mismatch. Did a clerical slip-up condemn Stefan?

Charlotte Kiszko, happy that the long crusade is over, hopes that the inquiry will also re-examine the original defence process at her son's trial. She is angry that Lord Waddington, a proponent of the death penalty, chose the defence he did for Stefan. She said: 'Suppose if we had capital punishment, would Stefan be dead now? I would like to string Waddington up by his

feet for an hour until he saw sense. Capital punishment is too barbaric an idea for a civilised country like this.

'They are talking now about compensation for what has happened, as much as half-a-million pounds, possibly. But how can any amount of money compensate for sixteen years spent in prison? I just want Stefan home, back where he belongs. If there is some money, perhaps he will go and visit his uncle in Australia. All I hope is that he will be well enough to live a normal life with me here. But we have to wait a few weeks to find out the truth of that.

'But you know what I think would be nice? I think if someone, somewhere, could give me an official apology for the terrible thing that happened to my son. No one has said sorry properly to me yet. Stefan tried very hard over the years to be positive and it is much easier for him to forgive than for me. It is in his nature. My main faith has always been him and I would have done anything to clear his name. I kept thinking through the years about his office colleagues, good state workers, and how they must have felt working alongside a murderer. I had to prove to them that he wasn't. Stefan's sentence was a life sentence for murder. I would have fought for ever if it had taken that long.'

Campbell Malone, to whom she owes so much, is not sure that the inquiry will ever bring out the full facts into this gross miscarriage of justice. He is not sure it was deliberate. He said: 'The police are very keen to get to the bottom of it because they feel it is a slur on the professionalism of all the police forces. But a lot of time has gone by, one of the most important people in the case, Jack Dibb, is dead and people's memories play tricks. What is certain is that anything that could go wrong with this case did go wrong.'

Above: *Charlotte Kiszko kisses the son who was so cruelly snatched from her after a tragic miscarriage of justice.*

ALFRED DREYFUS
A Shameful Case

All Alfred Dreyfus wanted was to serve his country, France. The establishment repaid his loyalty by branding him a spy, imprisoning him for five years and subjecting him to three rigged trials. The case still arouses both shame and passion.

Like no case before it or after it, the Dreyfus affair – or 'L'affaire', as it became known – shattered the morale of France and left a lasting stain on the national character. An exemplary French officer, Captain Alfred Dreyfus, attached to the French General Staff, was accused in 1894 of selling secrets to his nation's enemy, Germany.

In a grotesque frame-up, made all the more sinister by blatant religious bigotry because Dreyfus was a Jew, he was court martialled, stripped of his rank and sentenced to Devil's Island, the notorious disease-infested penal colony where death was the only release. At one time Parisian mobs clamoured in the streets and screamed for his execution as Dreyfus fever gripped every strata of society.

Only world opinion and the strivings of a few good men, spurred on by an unbending belief in his innocence, finally secured justice for Dreyfus and eventually succeeded in reversing a great miscarriage of justice. But what happened to Dreyfus sank deep into the French consciousness and it remains a national shame that the society that proclaimed liberty, brotherhood and equality in the 1789 revolution will never entirely shrug off.

Alfred Dreyfus was born into a wealthy family in Mulhouse in the French region of Alsace-Lorraine, on the borders with Germany, on 9 October 1859. His father was a textile merchant who had created a fortune and, through shrewd management and investments, ensured that Alfred and his other sons would be well looked after in life, no matter what careers they choose.

For Alfred, however, there was only ever one love in his life – the military. His sense of the greatness of France, 'La Gloire', motivated his desire to serve as an officer in its army, and, in 1880 he entered the 14th Regiment of Artillery as a 2nd Lieutenant after a stint at a military college. By this time France was licking her wounds, the nation still in a mortal state of shock, after the war with Prussia in 1871 which led to the humiliating defeat of France and the abdication of Emperor Napoleon III. In a lightning war which routed the French forces, Prussia took over Alsace-Lorraine and with it Dreyfus's home city. Determinedly, almost obsessively French, Alfred and his family moved to Paris after the defeat rather than live under the Hohenzollern eagle.

Opposite: *Alfred Dreyfus with his two young children. He was both an honourable soldier and family man, but he was also a Jew and for this, he was besmirched and damned.*

Below: *The famous newspaper article by the author, Emile Zola, that shamed the French Army and the government into the reinstatement of Dreyfus' honour and good name. The photograph shows Mathieu Dreyfus, Alfred's brother who fought relentlessly to prove his innocence.*

HIS SENSE OF THE GREATNESS OF FRANCE, 'LA GLOIRE', MOTIVATED HIS DESIRE TO SERVE AS AN OFFICER IN ITS ARMY.

As a young artilleryman, Dreyfus rapidly proved himself a military talent destined for great things. By 1889 he had achieved the rank of Captain, married a woman called Lucie Hadomard, to whom he was devoted, and become the loving father to two children. He had an austere bearing, although not given to too much close intimacy with his brother officers, he was kind and considerate, an officer and a gentleman in every way who devoted himself to his country, his work and his family.

Above: *Officers parade the accused Dreyfus into court.*
Below: *Scenes from Zola's trial for libel.*

anti-Semite who despised what he perceived as the aloofness of Dreyfus on the staff, claimed the letter had been recovered from the wastepaper basket of Lt Col Max von Schwartzkoppen, military attache at the German embassy in Paris, by a cleaner named Bastian who was one of Henry's own spies. The letter was in French, torn in four and detailed information on several military matters, including the hydraulic braking system of a 120mm gun, new artillery tactics and French troop strength on the island of Madagascar.

Anti-Semitism in France at the time was rife; several prominent Jewish politicians had been involved in a scandal surrounding the bankruptcy of the Panama Canal company. In such a climate of hysteria and loathing it was awkward to be a Jew in the army. Alfred Dreyfus was a man in the wrong place at the wrong time. Suspicions that he may have been the sender of the *bordereau*, because he was an artillery

A MODEL OFFICER

He was nominated for an attachment to the General Staff. The staff was the highest accolade for an ambitious young officer, the pinnacle of the French military machine that was seeking ways to restore the morale, reputation and, more importantly, the fighting effectiveness of the army after the debacle of 1871. He joined as a probationer on 1 January 1893 and for more than a year served as a model officer. But during this year there were alarming, ever increasing leaks of information about new weapons, defensive forts and tactics to the enemy across the Rhine. Dreyfus's life collapsed with the discovery of a memorandum, or *bordereau* which inexplicably turned up in the offices of the Statistical Section of the War Ministry offices in the Rue St Dominique on 27 September 1894.

Just five officers served in this small ministry, including Major Hubert Henry of the French Intelligence Service. Henry, an

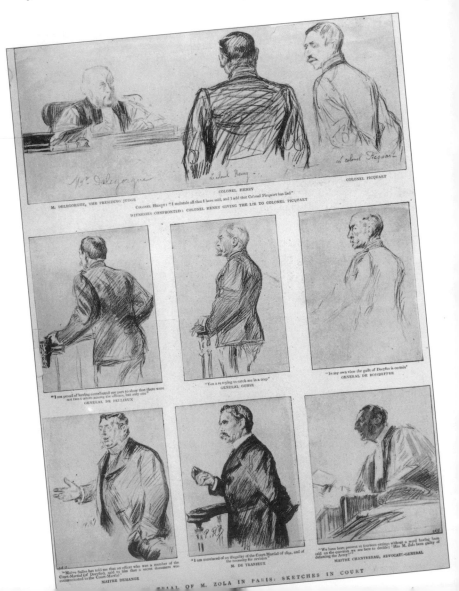

expert who had access to the information contained in it, soon became accepted fact without any proof at all. He was blamed because of his distance from his fellow officers, his lack of humour, because of his Jewishness and because he was the odd man out. Soon all the less-than-circumstantial evidence was believed to point to Dreyfus as the guilty party. Handwriting experts – all associates or friends of the

---

GUTTER NEWSPAPERS TOOK THE OPPORTUNITY TO USE THE PANAMA SCANDAL AS REASON TO CALL FOR THE REMOVAL OF ALL JEWS FROM PUBLIC LIFE IN FRANCE.

Charged with high treason, the family of Dreyfus, who never wavered in their belief of his innocence, cast about for the best lawyer they could find. They settled on Edgar Demange, an elderly, highly respected Catholic lawyer who told them: 'Should I find the least reason to doubt his innocence I shall not defend him. This will be known and commented upon. In fact, I shall be his first judge.' When he saw that all the evidence amounted to one *bordereau,* and the petty suspicions of the General Staff of a man they considered to be 'outside the fold' he was dumbstruck. He was confident that he could tear their case to shreds in a court of law.

On 18 Deceember 1894, the night before his trial began, Dreyfus wrote to Lucie, saying: 'Tomorrow I shall stand before my judges, upright and at peace with myself. I have nothing to fear.'

But the madness of mob hysteria was already gripping France and right-wing newspapers ran editorials pleading for the death penalty before his case had even been heard. In such a climate Dreyfus went

General Staff officers – concluded that a handwriting specimen from Dreyfus matched the writing on the *bordereau,* although even to the untrained eye they were patently very different.

Dreyfus was arrested and imprisoned on 15 October 1894. His chief inquisitor during preliminary investigations was Major Armand-Auguste-Ferdinand-Marie Mercier du Paty de Clam, an officer every bit as pompous as his lengthy name would suggest. Louis Snyder, in his scholarly study of the Dreyfus affair 'The Dreyfus Case', said: 'A cousin of the chief of staff, he was a blundering and erratic busybody who felt himself honoured by the assignment. A man of fertile and cruel imagination, he had the soul of a medieval inquisitor and was a violent anti-Semite.'

For seventeen days he continued a baffling and perplexing interrogation of Dreyfus, the man he considered the 'outsider within the fold' because of his Jewishness. 'That my brain did not give way,' Dreyfus wrote, 'was not the fault of the Commandant du Paty.'

Above, top: *The case was revised in 1899 at this court in Rennes. This revision was as unjust as his trial.*

Above: *The fake letter that was the chief evidence against Dreyfus and some of those involved against him.*

to trial the next day at the Rue Cherche-Midi, near the prison where he was held.

Seven officers were elected as judges at the court martial that the defence tried but failed to open to the public. Dreyfus knew it was in his interests to have the press and public there but he was powerless to bend the will of the court. Dreyfus set out his testimony: that it was impossible for him to

Henry, who was a relative of the court-room judge, suggested that he, Henry, be called with some new information. Taking the stand, he said he had received information the previous March, and again in June, from a man he called 'impeccable' but whom he refused to name that there was a traitor on the General Staff leaking secrets to Germany. Turning to Dreyfus with a theatrical flourish he pointed and said in a booming voice: 'There is the traitor!'

THE SECRET IDENTITY OF AN INFORMER

In plain violation of Article 101 of the Military Code which stipulated that an accused man had the right to know the identity of his accuser, the judge ruled that Henry did not have to name the person who had supplied him with this dubious intelligence. All Henry said was that it was a 'person of integrity' and, touching his hat, added: 'There are secrets in the head of an

have the information on the hydraulic braking system mentioned in the incriminating *bordereau* because he had never had access to it; that he knew nothing about Madagascar and that he was completely happy to serve the French army patriotically and undemandingly. He was rich, and did not need to sell secrets for money, and that if he had preferred the army of the Kaiser to that of the Second Republic, he would have returned to his native Alsace.

Three handwriting experts were summoned as the first witnesses. Two said the handwriting in the memorandum matched correspondence taken from Dreyfus's home, a third launched into a preposterous, totally bewildering account of how he had determined by scientific processes – which no one present could possibly fathom – that Dreyfus had merely disguised his handwriting in the *bordereau* to look different, but that it was really his. The evidence was looking so thin, so flimsy, that one senior War Ministry official reported to his superiors that it seemed likely that Dreyfus would be acquitted. That is, until the infamous Major Henry stepped in to nobble Dreyfus permanently with what has proved historically to be one of the most pernicious lies ever told in a courtroom.

officer that are kept even from his kepi.' Adding insult to this injury was a letter handed to the judge by the pompous Major Mercier du Paty de Clam who detailed within it his interrogation results. It was a document filled with lies and innuendoes, claiming that Dreyfus had been disloyal in the past and had, while at Bourges military academy, sold the Germans secrets of a new explosive. What he failed to say was that the Germans had been given the secrets of the new melanite shell before Dreyfus even attended the academy. Again, the contents of this appalling document were denied to his defence lawyer.

On 22 December, four days after the kangaroo court began sitting, the accused was led out of court for the reading of the verdict. He was found Guilty of treason and condemned to dishonourable discharge from the army, deportation from France and exile for life 'in a fortified place'. Demange, the honourable lawyer, wept with the injustice of it all.

Following his conviction came the public humiliation for Dreyfus. The press whipped the mob frenzy to fever pitch and thousands gathered in the great cities of France for weeks in rallies to demand his execution. He had become the scapegoat for all ills, including the French loss of the 1871 war, even though he was just twelve at the time of the French defeat. On 5 January 1895, at the Champ de Mars, the parade ground of the Ecole Militaire, a great crowd gathered, chanting 'Death to the Jew' as Dreyfus was led out before men representing each regiment in Paris. General Darras of the French Cavalry announced: 'Alfred Dreyfus, you are unworthy of carrying arms. We herewith degrade you in the name of the people of France.' With that a giant sergeant walked up to Dreyfus, tearing the epaulettes of rank from his shoulders, shredding the red stripes denoting his attachment to the General Staff from his trousers and snapping his officer's sword in two.

DREYFUS CRIED OUT, 'SOLDIERS! AN INNOCENT IS DISHONOURED. LONG LIVE FRANCE!'

In desperation Drefus cried out, 'Soldiers! An innocent is dishonoured. Long live France!' From the mob which had poured into witness this spectacle came an answering roar: 'Death to the Jew!' As he was paraded before the soldiers and the mob he stopped before a cluster of newspapermen and said to them in a soft voice: 'You will say to the whole of France that I am innocent.' On 17 December, after contemplating suicide in his cell over his hopeless situation, he was shipped off to Devil's Island, the former leper colony, but by now a remote, brutish hell-hole of a prison off the coast of French Guiana.

On Devil's Island he was forbidden to work, write and receive letters and even forbidden to look upon the sea, lest he somehow should contrive a means of toss-

Above: *The military prison in Rennes where Dreyfus was held.*

Left: *Captain Dreyfus on the left, leaves the War Office in Rennes during preliminary investigations before his trial. He is with an unidentified officer.*

Opposite, above: *Dreyfus stands before the tribunal in Rennes.*

Opposite, below: *Emile Zola, the author who fought to free Dreyfus.*

ing a bottle or some other message out on to the waves. Not even his guards were allowed to talk to him. In France his name was never mentioned in the Chamber of Deputies and Jews, who continued to suffer increased public persecution, all blamed the despicable actions of Dreyfus.

A single courageous French officer, Lt Col George Picquart, was determined never to forget the memory of his friend. He always believed in his innocence and was determined to find the guilty cuplrit.

Below: *The military paraded in honour of Dreyfus' re-instatement in 1906, but he had suffered the shame of having his sword broken and his freedom taken.*

In March 1896, fifteen months after Dreyfus was sentenced, a second torn note was again found in the German embassy, this one addressed to a Major Ferdinand Walsin-Esterhazy. Esterhazy, a French-Hungarian nobleman was a brave officer who had served with distinction in the war against Prussia, but was a reckless gambler who had squandered most of his family's fortune. Esterhazy was chronically in debt and almost always involved in one shady business deal after another; Picquart vowed to keep an eye on him. The torn letter was not proof of treason – it contained no military references – but its arrival and its source convinced Picquart that he had found the real traitor.

Picquart had been present at the Dreyfus trial but had been denied access to any written document other than the *bordereau*. He wanted to get hold of a handwriting sample of Esterhazy's – and good luck came his way when a month later Esterhazy, ambitious for more rank, status and money, applied for a position on the General Staff. Comparing his application to the notorious *bordereau*, Picquart discovered that the handwriting on each was almost identical. He showed it to several senior members of the staff who scrutinised it in turn. One, General de Boisdeffre saw it, saw the original memorandum which condemned Dreyfus, heaved a sigh and said: 'Well, we were wrong, weren't we?'

A HUMILIATING ADMISSION OF FAILURE

But it was by no means the end of the ordeal for Dreyfus. Esterhazy was a close friend of the despicable Major Henry, the man who had testified at the trial about a trusted stranger who had whispered of treachery, and whose name he could not reveal. It was becoming plain to Picquart that Major Henry had probably recognised the identity of the *bordereau's* author all along, and that he had framed Dreyfus in order to save his friend the gambler, Esterhazy. When Picquart confronted him with the handwriting Henry accused him of trying to stir up trouble to save 'that damn Jew'.

And that was the attitude of his superiors, too. In their view, the Dreyfus case was closed. The *bordereau* belonged to the Dreyfus case. If Esterhazy was found guilty

Soon the newspapers were clamouring for more blood and the French high command had no choice but to put Esterhazy on trial. As the Dreyfus hearing was a mockery of law, so was that afforded to his brother officer – only the outcome was different. In a two-day hearing on 10 and 11 January, 1898, Esterhazy was cleared of all charges by a corrupt court that again sat in secret and steamrollered all rules and protocal, including the right of Dreyfus' attorney to sit in and listen to the evidence. It became abundantly clear, even to the staunchest defenders of France's military clique, that something was rotten with the very fabric of the army.

The verdict in the court martial exploded in an historic front page of the newspaper L'Aurore on 13 January, 1898, written by the eminent novelist Emile Zola. Entitled 'J' Accuse' – 'I Accuse' – he risked criminal charges by publicly denouncing the military men, the system they shielded behind and calling for all Frenchmen in the abysmal case to stand up and be counted.

of peddling military secrets in the future then he would be tried. But not on the evidence that convicted Dreyfus. The military caste wanted to preserve their reputation and they could not suffer the humiliation that an admission of failure in the case of Dreyfus would bring upon them. Picquart was dumbstruck and vowed, in a shouting match with one superior, that he would never rest until Dreyfus was cleared.

Esterhazy was silenced by being sent out of France on missions, including examining the intelligence services on France's eastern border. They were assignments intended to stop him from rocking the cozy, closeted world of the staff any further. Major Henry went so far as to forge more crude letters, allegedly traitorous missives signed by the hand of Dreyfus, which mysteriously turned up. But Mathieu Dreyfus, the imprisoned officer's brother, learned of Picquart's discoveries and publicly denounced Esterhazy.

Above: *Colonel Schwarzkoppen (top), who was supposed to be Dreyfus's German spy master and journalists at the trial .*

Addressed to the President of the Republic, it read in part: 'A court martial has but recently, by order, dared to acquit one Esterhazy – a supreme slap at all truth, all justice! And it is done; France has this brand upon her visage; history will relate that it was during your administration that such a social crime could be committed. Since they have dared, I too shall dare. I shall tell the truth because I pledged myself to tell it if justice, regularly empowered, did not do so fully. My duty is to speak – I have no wish to be an accomplice.'

He went on to denounce Mercier du Paty de Clam and the military who had dragged France's name through the mud, condemning their secrecy and their passionate, obstinate protection of their own kind at the expense of an innocent man locked in a hellish jail thirteen thousand miles from France.

Left: *The hut and guard tower on Devil's Island where Dreyfus was held.*

Centre: *Devil's Island in relation to its neighbours.*

Below: *Bernard Lazarre, centre, was a staunch supporter of Alfred Dreyfus.*

Nevertheless, the military tried again, with the connivance of government officials, to put Dreyfus on trial one more time. His family and supporters were convinced that this time he would be exonerated and the shame of his conviction and banishment lifted for good. Once more, however, the shallow, evil but powerful men triumphed over the good.

Dreyfus arrived back in France, his sentence quashed and in the uniform of an artillery captain, to stand trial again in a court martial convened at Rennes. This time it was public, it lasted for thirty-three days, heard one hundred and fifteen witnesses and still regarded the litany of lies told by senior staff officers as the truth. At the end of the trial Dreyfus said in an impassioned speech: 'I only want to say to the country and the army that I am innocent. I have endured five years of horrible martyrdom to save the honour of my name and that of my children. I am certain that through your honesty and your sense of justice I shall succeed today.' Two hours later, by a verdict of five to two, he was again found Guilty of high treason but, due to 'extenuating circumstances', he was ordered to serve ten years instead of life.

A shocked world reacted with a barrage of outrage against France. In America the

Zola concluded: 'I have one passion only, for light in the name of humanity, which has borne so much and has a right to happiness. My burning protest is only the cry of my soul. Let them dare carry me to the court of appeal, and let there be an inquest in the full light of day! I am waiting.'

The force of the Zola article reverberated through the corridors of power. His masterful attack was called by the author Anatole France 'a moment in the conscience of mankind' as it sought to reverse the great injustices heaped upon the unfortunate Dreyfus. But before there was justice, there was revenge. The establishment closed ranks against Zola, charged him with libel, struck his name from the roll of the Legion of Honour and drove him into exile in London for a year. Their revenge was petty and short lived; soon the cause of Dreyfus was taken up by other important intellectuals and writers, among them Leon Blum, Jean Jaures and the man who would one day be premier of France, Georges 'The Tiger' Clemenceau.

On 19 September, 1899, Dreyfus left prison and the last stage of the campaign to clear his name began in earnest. In May 1906, the appeal court judges in Paris finally quashed the conviction of the court martial at Rennes, saying they were convinced that Dreyfus had been framed all along. He was restored to full rank in the army and his named was – rightly – added to the roll of the Legion of Honour.

On 22 July 1906, a military parade took place as he was given the award, France's highest for merit. Troops who twelve years before had paraded as his sword was broken and his rank badges stripped from him, now stood in salute. A huge crowd of two hundred thousand gathered spontaneously in the streets, screaming 'Long Live Dreyfus! Long Live Justice!' Tears of relief and joy streamed down his face as Dreyfus clutched his son Pierre to him.

Esterhazy, the villain of the piece, retired to England where he lived in poverty and shame in a slum area of London. He was spurned by the country he betrayed and died in poverty in 1923, having confessed

French flag was burned in the streets, a movement was started to boycott the great exhibition scheduled for the coming year. Queen Victoria was not amused and expressed publicly her hope that next time the poor martyr Dreyfus would be able to appeal to better judges.

The president of France wanted to pardon him, but Dreyfus and his supporters knew that a pardon would be an admission of guilt; to be pardoned of something you had to have done something in the first place. But his mental and physical state weakened, Dreyfus accepted the pardon, issuing the following statement: 'The government of the Republic gives me back my freedom. It means nothing to me without honour. From today I shall continue to seek reparation for the atrocious judicial error of which I am still the victim. I want the whole of France to know by force of final judgement that I am innocent. My heart shall be at peace only when there shall not be a single Frenchman who can impute to me the crime which another committed.'

Above: *The guard of dishonour as Dreyfus is led to prison. The troops turn their backs because they are forbidden to look at the traitor.*

Above, top: *An elderly but honoured Dreyfus can be seen weeping at the funeral oration for Zola.*

to a newspaperman that he had been the author of the infamous *bordereau* all along. Dreyfus served gallantly in the First World War, earning decorations for his actions at the Chemin des Dames and Verdun. He died after a long illness in bed on 11 July 1935, his legacy was the courage he displayed; his life was proof that an individual can take on the madness of wholesale corruption and triumph.

JOHN DEMJANJUK
Ivan the Terrible

Is the retired car-worker from Cleveland really Ivan the Terrible, the butcher of Treblinka? How would it feel to stand before an Israeli court accused of the most terrible crimes of the century? The jury is still out on John Demjanjuk.

Treblinka. To the very few who survived it, the name of the Nazi death factory is enough to bring back the most terrible memories, for it was one of the extermination centres designed to process those considered enemies of the Third Reich. Between 1942 and 1943, when the camp was razed to the ground in favour of the more efficient camps Auschwitz and Maidanek, Treblinka 'processed' nearly one million souls.

These so-called enemies of the Reich, brought from all over the conquered territories, were unloaded from cattle wagons and driven into the gas chambers filled with carbon monoxide gas from massive petrol engines. On their path to oblivion stood a man whose sadism has been described by one survivor as 'something so terrible, so inhuman, that he could not be called a creature of this planet.'

As the naked women filed into the death chamber this man hacked off their noses and their breasts with a sword. He casually bashed in men's skulls with lead piping and flayed prisoners with a whip knotted with iron balls. On his tour of the camp huts, where the living dead were kept working for the Reich for as long as it suited their masters, he drilled into men's buttocks with a carpenter's tool and shot the agonised victim if they cried out. The prisoners called him Ivan the Terrible.

Investigators came for a retired car factory worker called John Demjanjuk in 1981 after several years investigation by America's Immigration and Naturalisation Service. Demjanjuk was a pillar of his community in Cleveland, Ohio, where he had lived since 1952 after arriving from war-torn Europe in search of a better life in the New World.

In August 1952 Demjanjuk – his first name is Ivan but he changed it upon his entry to the USA – was hired for the princely sum equivalent to 90 pence an hour working on the production line at the Ford Motor Company plant. After toiling in the engine department of the factory he was promoted to a foreman's job. His wife, Vera, found work at a local General Electric plant and both diligent workers would stay with their respective employers until the day they retired.

The Demjanjuks had a son and a daughter – John Jnr and Irene – and lived in the Cleveland suburb of Parma before they saved enough money to move to the more affluent neighbourhood of Seven Hills. Every Sunday morning was spent at St Vladimir's Orthodox Church, the core of Ukrainian ex-patriate life in Cleveland. To

'SOMETHING SO TERRIBLE, SO INHUMAN, THAT HE COULD NOT BE CALLED A CREATURE OF THIS PLANET.'

Opposite: *John Demjanjuk who may be the victim of a ghastly KGB frame-up that branded him as a monster from the concentration camps.*

Below: *A pass that was supposed to have been issued in 1942 by the Nazi SS was used to identify Demjanjuk some forty years later.*

West believe him to be the victim of an old-style KGB frame-up; a frame-up designed and executed in the days before the collapse of communism. The people who believe in his innocence say that the evidence against him is circumstantial at best. Those who believe he is guilty are relying on the testimony of people who witnessed crimes committed fifty years ago. The fact that the Israeli Supreme Court is now giving credence to Soviet files – files released after the fall of the Communist system in Russia – means that doubt has been cast on his wartime role and upon the conviction. For the readers of this volume, here is the challenge of the evidence as presented on both sides – you be the jury on the most controversial war crime trial that has been staged since the end of the Second World War.

THE CASE FOR THE PROSECUTION

Ukrainian-born Ivan Demjanjuk first came to the notice of the US Justice Department in the late Seventies when a pro-Soviet journalist from the Ukraine arrived in New York brandishing a list which he said contained the names of more than seventy Nazi collaborators from the war years who now resided comfortably in America. The journalist handed the list to the Immigration and Naturalisation Department which went through its files on the people named. The list alleged that one Ivan Demjanjuk had

all who knew them and befriended them, the Demjanjuks were the perfect family.

But the FBI came for John Demjanjuk and shattered this harmless life. They came for him on the pretext that he had entered the country illegally. He had: he lied on his documentation that he was Polish and not Ukrainian, fearing, he said, that he might be sent back to the USSR of Stalin. But the INS were not really interested in a small lie on paper three decades before. They came for him because they believed he was Ivan the Terrible, the monster of Treblinka.

John Demjanjuk was tried, convicted and sentenced to hang by an Israeli court for his role in the biggest mass murder in history. At the time of writing, his conviction is still under appeal. It is too early to say whether or not he is guilty – but some of the most distinguished legal minds in the

served as a guard at the Nazi concentration camp of Sobibor. The INS in turn sent the picture taken of Demjanjuk at the time of his entry to the United States to Israeli police, along with the photographs of fifteen other suspects.

Ivan Demjanjuk was born on 3 April 1920, in the Ukraine village of Dub Macharenzi. Both his parents were disabled – his father from wounds received in the First World War and his mother from pneu-

*Opposite, top: **The defence claimed this was an authentic photo of Demjanjuk, a policeman not an SS guard.***

*Opposite, below: **Demjanjuk in handcuffs charged as a war criminal in Israel.***

later artillery training. He was wounded in fighting near the Dnieper River by a German shell and needed emergency treatment to remove a large sliver of shrapnel from his back. By 1942 he was fighting in the Crimea where superior German forces captured him and his unit. It is this point that the two versions of what happened to Ivan Demjanjuk part company.

The prosecution contend that he was taken to a POW camp at Rovno –

monia. Life was hard in the Soviet dominated republic where there was never enough food and schooling was limited. He moved to Moscow as a boy when Stalin's agricultural collectivisation policies created a famine that killed ten million people, but soon he was back in his village after his father failed to find work. 'My father sold his house for the equivalent of eight loaves of bread,' he said, 'and we went to Moscow. We ate the bread and were forced to return to nothing.' Luckily, in his teens, he gained employment as a tractor driver on one of the state farms and in 1938, in a bid to increase his chances of promotion, he joined the Komsomol, the Communist youth organisation.

In 1941 Hitler launched Operation Barbarossa, the conquest of the east. Demjanjuk was called up, given basic and

*Above: **A US immigration photo of Demjanjuk dated 1951 (left). On the right, a photo said to date from 1947 and taken at Flossenburg, East Germany. There is dispute that both of these are images of the same man, Demjanjuk, the alleged 'Ivan the Terrible'.***

THEY CAME FOR HIM ON THE PRETEXT THAT HE HAD ENTERED THE COUNTRY ILLEGALLY.

Demjanjuk himself confirms this – where he willingly volunteered to serve the Nazis. It is to the eternal shame of the Ukrainian people that her citizens were found, by the Nazis, to be among the most willing servants of the Reich. Ukrainians were found guarding the concentration camps, operating the gas chambers, enforcing Jewish round-ups in ghettos across the conquered territories. The prosecution contended that he was taken to a Nazi training camp at Trawniki, near the Polish city of Lublin, where he was issued with a uniform, a rifle and given SS identification in the form of a Wehrpass, or identity card. His blood group was tattooed under one arm, standard SS procedure. He was recruited for the sole task of service in the death camps.

From Trawniki, the prosecution contends that he moved to Treblinka where he

Right: *The many faces of Ivan the Terrible according to the prosecution: from top left, as Red Army soldier; camp picture, Trawniki; Flossenburg 1947; wedding picture 1948; immigration image 1951; daughter's wedding 1981 and at his trial in Israel.*

Below: *An electronic image mixing Trawniki photo of Demjanjuk with a current photograph.*

operated the machinery of death that 'processed' eight hundred and fifty thousand human beings. Here he excelled in pain and suffering, inflicting cruelties on his fellow-man that made his Nazi superiors baulk. They say that his limited intelligence was fuelled by rampant anti-Semitism – his birthplace was a known centre of anti-Jewish feelings.

After his immigration photo was sent to Israel it was shown to potential witnesses. After several positive identifications, an advertisement was placed in Tel Aviv newspapers seeking survivors from the camps of Sobibor and Treblinka to come forward. The Israeli authorities also asked for similar assistance in identifying another war crimes suspect from Miami, one Feodor Fedorenko, who later admitted he had served as a guard at Sobibor, albeit a reluctant one, and denied that he had ever taken part in atrocities. (Later Fedorenko was acquitted by a Miami judge of war crimes at his denaturalisation trial on the grounds that Jewish survivors were 'coached' into identifying him. Ultimately, however, a new hearing on appeal returned Fedorenko to the Soviet Union where he was executed by firing squad for war crimes. America, with its powerful and large Jewish population, among them survivors of the Nazi terror, intensely dislikes war criminals in its midst.)

After the Jewish survivors had identified Demjanjuk as their tormentor inside

Treblinka, he was interviewed by the Cleveland US Attorney's office to give a statement which he declined to do on the advice of his lawyer. A year later, after weighing up the Israeli evidence which included verification of an SS identity card, the Justice Department stepped in and filed a federal complaint against him.

In 1981 he went on trial to be denaturalised as a citizen, the first step in deporting him either to the Ukraine or to the Israeli authorities who now viewed him as a major war criminal. In June 1981, after hearing heart-rending testimony from survivors who swore that the man before them was Ivan the Terrible, Judge Frank Battisti ruled that 'the defendant was present at Treblinka in 1942 and 1943 and should therefore be stripped of his citizenship.'

Judge Battisti singled out the evidence of a man called Otto Horn, the only German SS man who stood trial for war crimes at Treblinka after the war to be acquitted. Horn, a humanitarian, served there as a nurse tending to SS staff and took no part in the massacres, although, controversially, some eyewitnesses claimed he took part in torturing inmates. American special investigator Norman Moscowitz showed him pictures of John Demjanjuk; he identified him as Ivan the Terrible.

AN INVESTIGATION OF PREJUDICE

On 18 October, 1983, Israel issued an arrest warrant for John Demjanjuk and a month later requested his extradition from America. Demjanjuk, fearful that he might be summarily executed if he was returned to the Soviet Union like Fedorenko had not thought of the possibility of facing justice in the Jewish homeland. For years he fought through every court in America. Appeal and counter-appeal failed until, on 28 February, 1986 he was flown to Tel Aviv to stand trial.

While he was held in an Israeli jail a crack team of Israeli prosecutors was assembled to methodically build the case against him. One of the men who would give evidence against Demjanjuk was Pinchas Epstein, a Jew in a working party at Treblinka who escaped in a revolt in the summer of 1943. In his shocking testimony, which he would later recount to the court, he said: 'I have nightmares... to this very day. One day a living little girl managed to get out of the gas chambers. She was alive. She was speaking. A girl of about twleve or forteen. People who took the corpses out of the gas chambers made her sit down on the side, and this little girl, her words ring in my ears still, she said: 'I want my mother'. Ivan took one young man from among us whose name was Jubas. He struck at him brutally with his whip. "Take your pants off" and with that he ordered him to rape the girl. This act was not performed and she

'THE DEFENDANT WAS PRESENT AT TREBLINKA IN 1942 AND 1943 AND SHOULD THEREFORE BE STRIPPED OF HIS CITIZENSHIP.'

was shot instead.'

When Ivan came to trial in 1987 there were four other survivors who took the stand after Epstein. Eliyahu Rosenberg's testimony was the most gripping. He described the terrible horrors he witnessed, the savagery with which Ivan hacked off pieces of bodies, of beating to death people with lengths of piping. When he came to identifying Ivan in the courtroom, Rosenberg said: 'Ivan. I say so unhesitatingly and without the slightest doubt. This is Ivan from the gas chambers. The man I am looking at. I saw his eyes. I saw those

Above: *Demjanjuk during his internment in Israel while the prosecution tries to prove that he is Ivan the Terrible from the Treblinka concentration camp. But the accused man insists that he is innocent.*

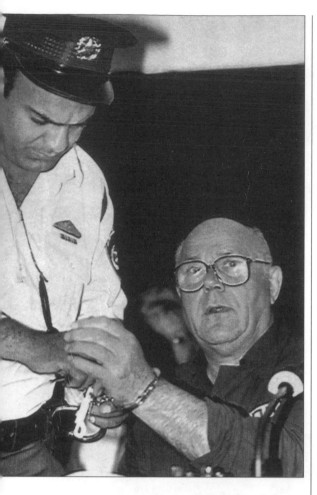

murderous eyes. I saw that face of his.'

The evidence of the eyewitnesses made moving testimony – testimony that defence lawyers for Demjanjuk were unwilling to call into question because of the enormity of the witnesses' suffering. But on top of the tearful identifications was the one key piece of physical evidence – the SS card bearing a photo of the young Ivan. Fully fifty days of the trial were spent assessing its authenticity, coming as it did from the Soviet Union which, in its time, pulled some mean stunts against enemies real and imagined. In the end the court decided that the card was authentic.

Judge Zvai Tal, handing down the ultimate penalty in May 1988, said: 'Demjanjuk served as a chief hangman who killed tens of thousands of human beings with his own hands. These crimes can never be forgiven in the minds or in the hearts of men. These crimes can never be obliterated from memory. It is as though Treblinka continues to exist, as though the blood of the victims still cries to us.' As the manacled Demnjajuk was led away the hysteriacl crowd was chanting ecstatically

ON TOP OF THE TEARFUL IDENTIFICATIONS WAS THE ONE KEY PIECE OF PHYSICAL EVIDENCE – THE SS CARD BEARING A PHOTO OF THE YOUNG IVAN.

Left and below: *The verdict was Guilty and the old man – Demjanjuk was seventy-two-years old at the time – was sentenced to death by the Israeli court. He was an ill man, and had to be wheeled into court. The verdict is still under appeal, and there is increasing evidence that Demjanjuk has been mistakenly identified and wrongly accused.*

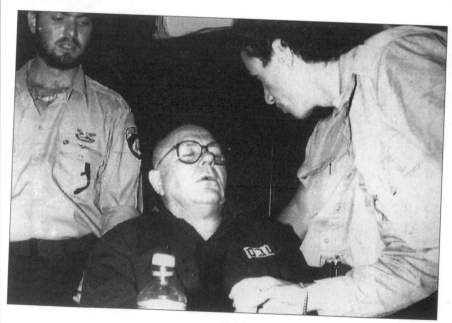

in Hebrew for his death.

THE CASE FOR THE DEFENCE.

John Demjanjuk argued an entirely different scenario to that offered up by his Israeli prosecutors. He agrees with events only as far as his capture in the Crimea. Then, he says, he was taken to the Rovno camp in Poland and transferred a few weeks later to the POW camp for Red Army captives in Chelm, Poland. Here, he claimed, he was put to work digging peat and moved on from there to another POW camp in Graz, Austria. It was at the Graz camp, he claimed, that he was given the tattoo under his arm to indicate his blood group – not, he said, because he was in the SS.

In 1945 he claimed the Germans offered him and his fellow Ukrainians the chance to join the Russian Liberation Army, an anti-Stalinist cadre. Because he, like other Ukrainians, felt little kinship for the Bolsheviks in Moscow, he says he agreed to join up, escaping at the end of the War to the west where he had the tattoo removed, an operation which left scar tissue. In 1945 he ended up at a displaced person's camp in Landshut, Germany, where he met Vera Kowlowa whom he would later marry and take to America for a new life.

On the stand at the trial his defence lawyers were hampered by their own inexperience in handling a war crimes trial and by Demjanjuk's inability to recall accurately his whereabouts in wartime. The SS identity card, he claimed, was a forgery –

as indeed, upon closer scrutiny, it might well be – and the eyewitnesses were mistaken over traumatic events that took place half-a-century earlier. Uneducated, still barely able to manage much English after close to four decades in America, his lawyers put down his inability to form a coherent defence to the charges to his lack of intellect. Either way, John Demjanjuk did not cut a convincing character in the dock and there were few surprises when he was found Guilty. But it seems, on appeal, that the case might finally swing his way.

It is thanks to the determined efforts of his son, John Jnr, and his son-in-law Ed Nishnic, that he might shake off the death sentence and prove beyond doubt that he is not Ivan the Terrible – even though it is conceivable he did work for the Nazis. After learning of their sleuthing through Kremlin files (which had become more accessible under glasnost and finally totally accessible after the fall of Communism in the summer of 1991), Gitta Sereny, the influential Italian journalist has pointed out: 'It is conceivable that the Israeli Supreme Court may now have to be content with Ivan the Less Terrible.'

'My father,' said John Jnr, 'was just your typical immigrant who came over on the boat trying to escape Communism and make a better life. Go into any Serbian or Ukrainian church and you'll meet a hundred like him. He is not a mass murderer. I would not give up my life for him if I ever thought he was.'

Thanks to amazing detective work – and some help from insiders on the government team who were sympathetic to the Demjanjuk side – John Jnr and Nishnic built up a credible dossier for his acquittal. One employee of the Office of Special Investigations, which carried out the Justice Department probe into Demjanjuk's life, went through garbage every week from the OSI bins. It was pieced together painstakingly by the two men in the basement of Demjanjuk's home. They learned, for instance, that Horn, the acquitted SS man, initially did not pick out Demjanjuk, then identified someone else and was then shown pictures selectively in a fashion calculated to make him point out Demjanjuk.

The appeal was put back eighteen months due to the suicide of one of his lawyers and an acid attack on another. But in that period Nishnic and John Jnr were not idle. In September 1990, John Jnr trav-

Above: *Demjanjuk is embraced by his son during the Israeli trial. His children have stood by Demjanjuk throughout and have even rallied tremendous support in the American Ukrainian community for their father. They are sure he is not Ivan the Terrible. Meanwhile, Demjanjuk (left) continues his brave battle to clear his name.*

elled with Yoram Sheftel, Demjanjuk's fierce and brilliant new lawyer (who was rewarded for his efforts to defend Ivan the Terrible with acid in his face that nearly cost him his sight) to the Crimea, in search of answers to riddles that took place a long time ago. They were promised the KGB file on the trial of Fedorenko... but then the KGB refused to hand it over. Ultimately, however, they contacted Alexander Yeemetz, a sympathiser in the Ukrainian Parliament who obtained a KGB file containing twenty-one confessions of former Treblinka guards – all of them Soviets – taken between 1944 and 1961.

Each statement identified Fedorenko.

Each statement said that the gas chamber was operated by Ivan the Terrible.

Each statement said that Ivan's surname was Marchenko.

In August 1991, after much legal wrangling, the file was accepted into evidence for the defence. Also accepted into evidence were the names and statements of a further forty Soviet guards and underlings of the Treblinka camp – each one of whom testifies that a man named Marchenko was the operator of the gas chamber. One of the statements is from a Nikolai Shelayev, who admitted to being one of the gas chamber operators along with Ivan Marchenko. He

---

'IT'S LIKE THEY CAN'T GET HIM ON ONE THING SO THEY WILL FISH AROUND UNTIL THEY GET HIM ON ANOTHER.'

Below: *John Demjanjuk has been away from home for over ten years, his life with wife and family shattered. Yet his case is seen increasingly as a dreadful error by the Israeli authorities, compounded by the fact that dubious KGB files have been used as evidence.*

---

says that in June 1943 he and Marchenko were moved to Trieste in Italy to guard political prisoners and that he last saw him the following year when he defected to communist partisans fighting for Tito in Yugoslavia. Shelayev was shot by the Soviets in 1951. He died without ever mentioning the name Demjanjuk.

More significantly, in documents obtained under America's Freedom of Information Act, Demjanjuk's crusading family learned that the Justice Department knew back in 1978, via a Soviet official called Pavel Leleko, that the duo who operated Treblinka's gas chamber were named Nikolai and Marchenko, and that Marchenko had a brutal penchant for severing women's breasts. This information on the man that the Demjanjuk family contend is Ivan the Terrible was never followed up.

Last year Nishnic went to the Ukraine in search of clues as to the background of Marchenko. He found his widow's apartment but was too late – she had died forty days before his arrival. His daughter in the city of Kryvy Rog said her father had gone off to war and had never come home again; she had never known him beyond infancy. But she promised to try to find a photograph of him; it was handed over to Nishnic in January 1992. When placed alongside Demjanjuk's picture the similarities are striking. Now the defence team are confident that the Guilty verdict can and should be overturned.

WHICH CRIMINAL? WHAT CRIME?

But Demjanjuk is so vague on his wartime record – and new files are being unearthed monthly – that it is likely that, although he will escape the death penalty, he may be punished for crimes he may or may not have committed. Israel has never gone after camp guards, the 'small fish' who were not involved in wholesale mass murder. But confronted by the new evidence which suggests that he is not Ivan the Terrible, prosecutors seem intent on making him guilty for other, unspecified crimes. For instance, if the SS identity card is genuine, it lists him being at Sobibor, another death camp. A Sobibor guard has sworn in a statement that he knew a Demjanjuk there.

Other documents from what was East Germany show that a Demjanjuk served at

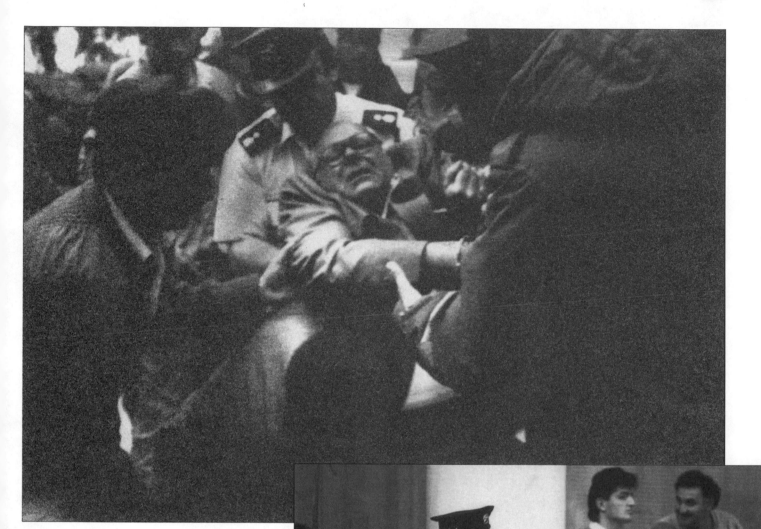

the Flossenburg concentration camp with the number 1393 – the number he was allegedly given at the Trawniki camp. However, nothing exists to link him with mass murder at these places. Dov Freiburg, one of only twenty living survivors of Sobibor, said: 'He must have been small fry otherwise I would have remembered him. If he had been one of the big-timers destroying people, I may have remembered him. It was all along time ago.'

Assistant prosecutor Dafna Bainvol seems to sum up the Israeli attitude when he said: 'We are going to prove to the Supreme Court that he is a Nazi who was at least in Sobibor and Flossenburg.'

At least – they are two words which smack of vengeance. However much the souls of the Nazi concentration camp victims cry out for it, justice is what is needed to preserve the memory of the Holocaust, not mindless vengeance.

John Jnr is outraged that his father should now face a different set of charges. 'It's like they can't get him on one thing so

Above: *In April 1988, John Demjanjuk had to be carried into court as his back was so very weak and painful. In court, he had had to listen to allegations that he was responsible for gassing more than 850,000 Jews and torturing countless more.*

they will fish around until they get him on another,' he said. If his father did admit to being a guard, and not being Ivan the Terrible, he says he could forgive him. He added: 'Would he have been morally wrong at the time, to choose the option of living over dying? Would he be any more culpable than the Jew who worked for the Nazis pulling gold teeth out of the mouths of victims after they had been gassed? I

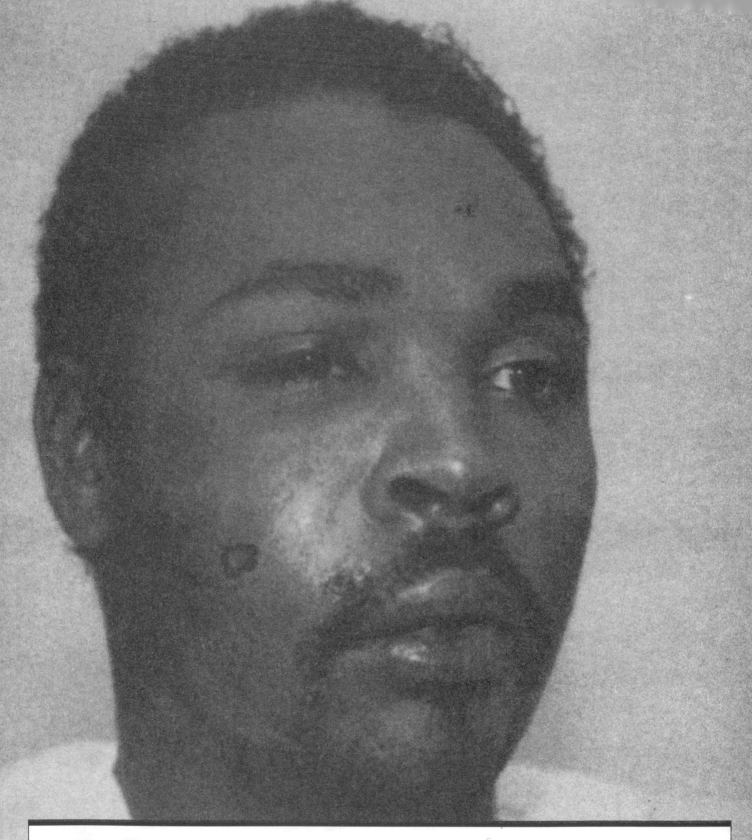

RODNEY KING
Denial of Evidence

When a jury refused to believe their own eyes, they set off a riot which left Los Angeles burning for days. The video tape of the vicious beating Rodney King received from the police had been broadcast around the world. Why were the policemen acquitted?

In his masterpiece '1984', George Orwell depicts a nightmare world of Big Brother, thought police and hate-ins, where his hero, Winston Smith, works in the Ministry of Truth where he re-writes history to suit his masters. Things that took place are altered so they never happened, black becomes white, white becomes black. Something frighteningly similar happened for real in Stalin's Soviet Union: subscribers to Russian encyclopaedias regularly received correspondence telling them to rip out the biographies of generals or statesmen who had been purged from the hierachy and officially no longer existed in the consciousness of the state.

The West has long held up such pernicious practices as the ultimate evil of authoritarian, communist tyrannies. But in May 1992, in America, the guardian of the free world where the rights of man are contained in a written constitution, it seemed that Winston Smith and his Ministry of Truth could have been at work in a courtroom north of Los Angeles.

In this courtroom, a jury decided that a videotape, which showed a black man being beaten and kicked repeatedly by police officers in a shocking orgy of brutality, was nothing more than 'legitimate force'. They ruled, with classic Orwellian logic, that the black man – motorist Rodney King – was 'controlling the situation' because of his attitude even as he lay helpless under the rain of blows. With the acquittal of the four police officers charged in the incident came the aftershocks of disgust and indignation. President Bush in the White House could not believe it and ordered FBI enquiries to bring fresh, civil rights violations against the accused policemen. But shock and outrage were not enough for the oppressed minorities in the ghettoes of LA who rose up in a two-day orgy of looting, burning and murdering. The City of Angels turned into a battleground as the fury over the King

verdict spilled on to the streets and against the police who were vindicated in a case where modern technology, in the form of a video camera, should have ensured there could be no vindication. At the end of the rioting – which spread to other cities – LA's South-Central district was a smoking ruin, swarming with armed troops and National Guards. Was there one justice system for whites and one for everyone else?

A BLACK MAN BEING BEATEN AND KICKED REPEATEDLY BY POLICE OFFICERS IN A SHOCKING ORGY OF BRUTALITY, WAS NOTHING MORE THAN 'LEGITIMATE FORCE'.

Above: *The acquittal of the policemen who beat King sparked riots and looting in Los Angeles.*

Opposite: *The bruised and beaten face of Rodney King after he encountered policemen who tried to stop him speeding in his car.*

The officers ultimately responsible for turning LA into a charcoal pit with 51 dead and billions of pounds worth of damage, couldn't have known what they were getting into when they stopped Rodney Glen King in his car on the night of 3 March 1991. King, no angel when it came to the law, was stopped for speeding. A convicted armed robber, a drug abuser, a man, in that classic phrase 'well known to the law', led officers of the Los Angeles Police Department on a terrifying, sometimes life-threatening high-speed chase on the freeway network of LA At times King was driving close to 100 miles per hour and there were real fears that he would kill innocent people if he lost control of the vehicle. Finally, King was forced to stop in a suburb of Los Angeles and surrounded by over a dozen cops from several squad cars, all with their guns drawn. King was a lethal suspect who had terrorised a corner store owner with a knife – the incident which led to his armed robbery conviction – police had every right to be wary of him. He was obviously drunk – and, for all the police arresting him knew, maybe stoned on drugs

HE WAS RECORDING A SLICE OF VIOLENT HISTORY THAT WOULD BECOME EVERY BIT AS IMPORTANT TO THE CIVIL RIGHTS MOVEMENT IN AMERICA AS THE BIRMINGHAM BUS BOYCOTT.

Below and opposite: *An amateur cameraman filmed a nasty scene of police brutality as the law officers beat and kicked King. The policemen claimed that they used only 'reasonable force' to subdue the man.*

like LSD or PCP, the latter known as 'Angel Dust' and a drug capable of giving a person superhuman strength combined with a loss of the sense of reality.

Rodney King's arrest would not even have made the newspapers had it not been for thirty-one-year-old plumbing store manager George Holliday who was on his balcony after midnight. Unable to sleep, he was experimenting with his new video recorder to see how it worked in poor lighting conditions. Suddenly, as he panned his camera around, he switched on the zoom lens as he caught sight of the police cars with their lights flashing. Illuminated in the headlights of the cars was a black man, his hands above his head. George Holliday did not know it at the time but he was recording a slice of violent history that would become every bit as important to the civil rights movement in America as the Birmingham bus boycott or the shooting of Martin Luther King.

His camera rolled for seven minutes – but it was eighty-one seconds from that seven minutes that shocked the world when George sold it for less than £300 the fol-

lowing day to a local TV network. In that eighty-one seconds, Rodney King, twenty-five, was subjected to over eighty-five blows from the batons of the police officers. At 12.52 am, roughly thirty seconds into the beating, King is seen struggling to his knees, his arms raised apparently in a gesture which says 'no more, no more'. He was hit twice by Taser stun-guns, which deliver 50,000 volts of electricity. At 12.53am he is seen still writhing under a rain of blows. Officer Theodore Briseno has his boot on King's neck. Ten seconds later he is motionless and *still* receiving blows from batons and kicks. Finally he is cuffed and dragged into a police car. He has sustained a broken ankle, skull fractures, a permanently damaged eye and needed two days of hospital treatment. 'What happened to you?' one doctor reportedly said to him. 'Fall down a set of stairs in the police station?' It was a throwaway line, but one with sinister overtones of what might happen to minorities if they fall into the hands of brutally and illegally violent LAPD police officers.

Newscasters at a TV station in Los Angeles where George Holliday sold his tape could not believe the explosive materi-al delivered into their hands. Clearly this was some of the most sensational amateur footage of a crime being committed – committed by the personnel entrusted to defeat and prevent crime – ever taken. When it was screened the effect across America was explosive. Coast to coast, civic leaders stepped forward to condemn what happened while the embattled Los Angeles Police Chief Darryl Gates struggled to put

TEN SECONDS LATER HE IS MOTIONLESS AND STILL RECEIVING BLOWS FROM BATONS AND KICKS.

Above: *Rodney King did not testify at the trial but in the wake of the verdict he stepped forward to deliver a halting, impassioned plea for peace as the city of LA burned.*

'IT WAS A WIERD FEELING AND I WAS TRYING TO THINK: "WHAT COULD HE HAVE DONE TO DESERVE THIS?"'

some kind of explanation to what was rapidly becoming an indefencible incident. Gates, a figure of controversy for many years – he once claimed blacks died in police choke holds because their physical make-up was different from that of whites – was even disowned by Los Angeles Mayor Tom Bradley. Bradley, a black man who was a former police officer, voiced the disgust and indignation of an enraged nation when he said: 'Clearly there will have to be an investigation so far reaching and so wide that no aspect of this disturbing and unsettling affair can be left unaccounted for. This is something we cannot and will not tolerate. I am as shocked and as outraged as anyone.' At first Gates suspended the four officers who dealt out the beating, but when it became clear that public outrage would settle for nothing less than criminal charges, the LA district attorney handed down charges.

The shadows who wielded the batons that night were identified as career officers. Sergeant Stacy Koon, forty-one, was in command that night. He was charged with assault with a deadly weapon, excessive force by an officer under colour of authority, filing a false police report and being an accessory to assault. Koon served in the Air Force and joined the LA police department in 1976. It would later come out that he shot and wounded a suspect who had fired on police after a drive-by shooting in 1989. The police commission commended him for his handling of the incident, but they were not so proud of his disciplinary hearings for excessive force while on the job. Married with three children, he plans to write a book about his experiences on patrol with the LAPD.

THE POLICE LOSE CONTROL

Theodore Briseno, thirty-nine, would later break ranks with his fellow cops during the trial and blame them for the beating. 'I just thought the whole thing was way out of control,' he claimed. Married with two children, he was charged with assault with a deadly weapon and excessive force by an officer under colour of authority. Theodore Briseno has been twice commended for bravery while on duty.

Laurence Powell would come to be painted as the bogeyman during the trial because he delivered most of the blows to King – thirty-three in all. When he was initially arraigned he said he thought King was on drugs and that 'I was completely in fear of my life. I was scared to death.' Powell, son of a Los Angeles Marshall, was twenty-nine at the time of his arrest and has been in trouble before with the force for excessive use of force. Salvador Castaneda, thirty-six, a robbery suspect, had his arm broken after being struck five times by Powell's baton. He was awarded £40,000 in a civil suit settlement last year. A police officer since 1987, Powell was charged with assault with a deadly weapon, excessive force by an officer under colour of authority and filing a false police report.

Timothy Wind, a thirty-two-year-old probationary cop, was the fourth man arrested and was fired by Chief Gates in the weeks following the beating because he did not have a contract with the city due to his rookie status. Accused of aggressively beating and kicking King he was also charged with assault with a deadly weapon and excessive use of force by an officer under colour of authority. He became a policeman a decade ago in Kansas and had only been in the LA force a short time when the King beating happened. He is also a married man with a young child.

George Holliday became a nationwide celebrity and appeared on TV talk shows with the regularity of a film star. He described how he was experimenting with his new camera on the terrace of his home twenty miles from downtown LA when he witnessed the dramatic end to the police chase. He couldn't believe his eyes when he saw the beating begin. He said: 'Before they started hitting him he was pretty much co-operative. It was a weird feeling and I was trying to think: "What could he have done to deserve this?"' Another eyewitness, Eloise Camp, said: 'I never saw him offer any resistance.' A third eyewitness, Dorothy Gibson, a fifty-two-year-old nurse, added: 'I could hear him pleading: "please

Below: *Righteous anger gave way to gratuitous and wanton destruction of property all across the city. Other racial tensions were expressed as blacks burned down Asian owned shops and homes.*

stop, please stop." He put his hands over his head to try to cushion the blows. After the beating was over the policemen were all just laughing and chuckling like they had just had a party.' The incident triggered a slew of instant TV and newspaper probes into previous allegations of Los Angeles police brutality. For once the mainstream media was alert and listening to numerous cases of brutality allegedly committed by police officers – most of which had gone unpunished. The accusations of inbred racism in the eight-thousand-four-hundred strong police department were further

Below and opposite:
Rodney King presented a dignified, yet emotional, public face. His obvious distress at the burning of his city touched many as he pleaded on television 'Can't we all just get along?' He became a symbol for something better than either the law or the mobs.

strengthened by the release of computer message transcripts sent from the police involved in the beating back to their headquarters that night. There were references to 'Gorillas in the Mist' and other racial slurs which only served to fuel the growing anger and resentment just bubbling beneath the surface of the population.

Karol Heippe, executive director of the Police Misconduct Lawyer's Referral Service, a national watchdog body which monitors incidents of police violence, said of the videotape: 'It's horrible. It's horrible, but I must say that we receive complaints in this office of that kind on a weekly, if not a daily basis. The difference is that this time there was somebody there to video-

> SLICK LAWYERS WHO ARGUED SUCCESSFULLY THAT WHAT THE JURY SEES ON THE TAPE IS NOT WHAT ACTUALLY HAPPENED.

tape it.' For the first time in American judicial history a videotape would be offered up to a jury as the only evidence for the prosecution. The camera couldn't lie, mused prosecutors, and they felt certain that a conviction for all four police officers was assured. But they hadn't reckoned on three things – a change of trial venue outside LA, a jury that was ready to side with authority rather than a convicted criminal and slick lawyers who argued successfully that what the jury *sees* on the tape is not what actually *happened*.

The trial was switched at the last moment to the Los Angeles suburb of Simi Valley. A judge decreed that switching the trial away from Los Angeles, where feelings were running high, would ensure a fairer trial. What in fact it did was to weigh the scales of justice heavily in favour of the defendants. By ordering the trial to take place in Simi Valley the judge was effectively placing them in the hands of jurors drawn from a suburb that is largely white, largely middle class and, crucially, drawn from a community that is the residence of choice for many LA police officers. The result was indeed a jury with just two ethnic minorities sitting on it and no blacks. Another factor was that the jurors had little awareness of how violent were racial confrontations between public and law officers had become in the big city where the very concept of law enforcement took on insidious and brutal connotations. The trial gave the cops the edge from the word go.

PLAY IT AGAIN, AND AGAIN, AND AGAIN

The trial opened a year after the assault – a year in which the wedge between black and white in Los Angeles was driven wider and deeper. All four officer pleaded Not Guilty to all the charges and it immediately became apparent that their defence strategy was going to be that they were within the law to use force to subdue their suspect. The video, now shown hundreds of times on TV, was about to be dissected and microscopically analysed by their lawyers – planting in the minds of the jury that the apparent random use of force against the hapless Mr. King was nothing of the kind – that it was in fact sustained, measured and controlled violence as laid down by the

LAPD guidelines for dealing with potentially violent prisoners. Michael Stone, the attorney for officer Powell said: 'When I first saw the tape my knees were shaking. I thought the frames, particularly those where King is on the ground and he is still being hit, put us in a terrible hole. But then I realised that there were positive things to point out. I figured with the other lawyers that the officer clearly complied with rules for escalating degrees of force. Police are trained to use their batons to cause pain. That usually stops a suspect. If it doesn't they are allowed to increase the level of pain and that's what these officers did. King is a big man and these officers were not going to allow him to get into a position where he could stand up again and perhaps pose an additional threat to them.'

NO EXPRESSION OF PAIN OR FEAR

Lawyer Darryl Mounger, himself an ex LA cop for ten years who was representing Sgt Stacy Koon, said: 'A little pain is a great incentive. When you get hit with a metal baton by someone who knows how to swing it, you're supposed to do what they say so they don't hit you again. The officers simply did what they are trained for, using the tools that they are given. A picture is worth a thousand words, but a lot of times it takes a thousand words to explain a picture. What you think you see isn't always what you see. King had a look of determination in his eyes. He did not have a look of pain or fear on his face.'

This was where unreality seemed to take over during the proceedings as the jury was, in the eyes of trial critics, literally brainwashed into thinking that the beating was exactly what King deserved, despite the fact he offered no resistance and posed no threat. The line of defence was that the police thought him capable of posing a threat to them and were correct in subduing him before that threat materialised. To many this was the equivalent of 'shoot first and ask questions later'. When it came to explaining why Officer Briseno had his foot on King's neck his lawyer John Barnett said: 'He may actually have saved King's life. Briseno isn't really attacking him but keeping him on the ground for his own good. In this late stage of this highly-charged confrontation maybe he could have

'THIS WAS CALIFORNIA, WITH IT'S EQUALITY LAWS AND ITS POSITIVE THINKING AND ITS INGRAINED, INBRED SENSE OF FAIR PLAY.'

got shot if he didn't stay down. That was what my client was doing.'

Despite the arguments from the lawyers it is fair to say that an air of inevitability hung over the courtroom. President Bush, who had already instructed FBI officers to look into possible civil rights violations, seemed as convinced as anyone of the outcome of the trial. The men were facing up to seven years each in jail, but it was likely that they would probably get a couple of years a piece, some of it suspended. There had developed in the psyche of the American public a belief that justice, in lib-

eral, progressive California, would be done in the shape of Guilty verdicts on all four men. 'This was not some redneck trial taking place in Alabama or some other deep south hell-hole where nigger-lynching was an accepted part of folklore,' wrote columnist Peter Melnitch. 'This was California, with its equality laws and its positive thinking and its ingrained, inbred sense of fair play. Nothing could prepare us for the verdict when it came down.'

The verdict came down on Wednesday 29 April 1992 and America – and later the world – was shaken to the core by it. The men were all found Not Guilty on all counts, save for officer Powell. The jury were deadlocked on one count of use of excessive force. Winston Smith and his Ministry of Truth had won – what had happened that night hadn't actually happened and what was seen on the video wasn't what actually had taken place. The jury had bought into a jargon-ridden defence which honoured the violence as being an 'acceptable' part of police procedures. The effect of the verdict was both instantaneous and

appealed for calm, admitted he was as staggered as anyone by the verdicts; even President Bush had to admit his surprise. But words were no longer sufficient for a mob who saw the acquittals as tacit approval for the LAPD to beat black men as and when they liked.

Throughout that first night LA burned as never before as the police totally lost the

Above and opposite:
Fires burned out of control and hard-pressed emergency services struggled to cope. LA was blanketed in a thick layer of soot. Planes could not land and many people suffered respiratory problems. And race relations were exposed as taut and hostile. The city has yet to recover from the physical and spiritual damage of those days.

tragic. The president in his Oval Office in Washington was informed immediately just as the flames from the first riots began to level whole sections of the City of Angels.

Soon America would witness scenes it hadn't seen on national television in decades. The all-consuming rage of a population in the ghettoes of Los Angeles, ground down by poverty and drugs, hopelessness and murders, rose up in fury at the 'white man's justice'. Whole city blocks in the South-Central district of the city, the teeming quarter that is home to blacks and poor Latinos, were consumed in the flames of madness. Tom Bradley, the mayor who

streets. Mobs screaming 'no justice, no peace!' marched on City Hall, on the courthouse, looting, torching and attacking any white face they saw. Although no justification can ever be found for the way the mob behaved, their spontaneous outburst of anger at so grotesque a miscarriage of justice jarred the nation to its roots. LA became a city under siege as the notorious gang-members in South-Central joined forces to wage war against cops and the city was placed under a dawn-to-dusk curfew. Still the fury wasn't played out and by dusk on the second day the city glowed anew with thousands of fresh fires. Mostly confined to the black ghettoes and downtown Los Angeles, the rioting spread to posh residential districts and many whites joined in the trouble which flared with the rapidity of a brush fire.

The fringes of Beverly Hills, one of the richest square miles of real estate on earth, was targeted by looters who ransacked a gem store, a clothes shop and torched a gym and there was also sporadic looting in wealthy upper-crust Westwood.

President Bush appealed for calm as the rioters continued to loot and destroy their ghettoes and areas near the downtown section of the city. Horrified TV viewers were stunned at the sight of marauding black lynch mobs stopping cars at random on the streets to drag the white occupants out for brutal beatings.

In perhaps the most graphic TV scenes a truck driver was pulled from his cab and his head smashed in with a tyre iron. As innocent Reg Denny staggered on to his hand and knees another black youth came by and kicked him with all his might in the head. Another stole his wallet as one of his assailants punched the air with glee. A helicopter-mounted TV camera captured the scenes of appalling brutality as the man staggered back into his truck and drove it for two blocks before he collapsed. Another man was seen with a pump-action shotgun peppering any passing cars that came within his field of fire.

The murderous rat-tat-tat of automatic weapons and the report of shotguns echoed throughout the night. Hospital emergency rooms were swamped with victims, many of them caught in cross fire. Twenty five primary school children were trapped in their classroom overnight as the flames from petrol bombs made them prisoners in the school at the heart of South Central Los Angeles. Many Korean stores – the resentment between blacks and Koreans has been simmering for years in American inner cities – were targeted by the mobs. Black shopkeepers, desperate to save their properties, hung signs saying 'black owned' in a bid to save them from the petrol bombers. By the time National Guardsmen and regular troops hit the streets LA looked like a war zone. There were fifty-one people dead, hundreds of injuries and property damage close to a billion and a half pounds. The city looked like a war zone.

THE MURDEROUS RAT-TAT-TAT OF AUTOMATIC WEAPONS AND THE REPORT OF SHOTGUNS ECHOED THROUGHOUT THE NIGHT.

AS INNOCENT REG DENNY STAGGERED ON TO HIS HAND AND KNEES ANOTHER BLACK YOUTH CAME BY AND KICKED HIM WITH ALL HIS MIGHT IN THE HEAD.

The jurors, many of whom sought police protection, justified their verdicts in anonymous interviews afterwards. Appalled by the mountain of indignation and scorn heaped on them, they claimed they were merely doing their duty within the framework of the law. One said: 'The only input I had was what the judicial system, the judge, the defence attorneys, the prosecutors gave me to work with – the law's the law.' Another said: 'The video was ludicrous. Clearly Rodney King was controlling the whole situation.' The disbelief that had settled in America over the acquittals went to the highest levels. President Bush announced shortly afterwards that the men would be back in court to face charges that King's civil rights were violated in the attack; clearly he was as outraged at the verdict as some of the people who took to the streets in the blood disturbances. At the time of writing the four accused have not yet had their second day in court.

Mayor Bradley spoke for all when he said: 'The jury's verdict will never blind us to what we saw on that videotape. The men who beat Rodney King do not deserve to wear the uniform of the LAPD, nor do any others who think what they did was right. The system failed us. We must do our best to ensure that it never fails us again.'

SIMON HAYWARD
An Officer And A Gentleman

Simon Hayward was a dashing Guards officer, the last man anyone expected to be involved in an international narcotics ring. He was jailed for five years but was it the right Hayward brother who was put behind bars? And where is brother Christopher now?

For newspaper reporters, it was a story too good to miss. When the first wire reports came through from Stockholm on Saturday, 14 March 1987, with their story that a British army officer, who used to guard the Queen on ceremonial duties, had been arrested near the Swedish capital and charged with drug running, Fleet Street dispatched hordes of newshounds to cover the unexpected case.

Simon Hayward, a dashingly-handsome career officer with a brilliant future ahead of him in his chosen regiment, the Guards, had seemingly thrown it all away for one hundred and eleven pounds of high-grade cannabis resin worth over £250,000 at street value. The cannabis was discovered by Swedish police hidden in false panels inside a Jaguar car. On the surface it seemed, to use a well-worn police phrase, that Simon Hayward was caught 'bang to rights'. In July that year in a Swedish court he was found Guilty of smuggling and sentenced to five years jail. But behind the simple act of smuggling lay a story of international intrigue, brotherly betrayal and a murderous international syndicate.

Simon Hayward is out of jail now and still sticking to his story that he was the innocent dupe of his wayward brother Christopher, a man with a history of drug use and abuse; a modern day Cain who betrayed his brother and never lifted a finger to help him when he became the fall guy. Sweden is a democratic country with fair laws and a judiciary independent of political control. And yet there are many who feel that Simon Hayward was a victim of a miscarriage of justice... and that, if Christopher Hayward ever reappears, he could be the man who could clear his brother's name.

Before he was branded a drug runner Simon Hayward had everything to live for. A captain at thirty-three, his rank and his charm gave him an entrée into the world of debutante balls, society dinners and exclusive holidays. A product of Wellington College in Crowthorne, in the heart of the English countryside, his masters knew from an early age that he was destined for great things. The son of an RAF officer who left the service to fly for a commercial airline, Simon Hayward was driven by two firm principles – honour and duty. He betrayed neither in the long years with the army and was entrusted with guarding his monarch when Simon was a resplendent horseman vigilant outside Buckingham Palace. It was a moment that Simon wished his father could have seen, but his mother Hazel held enough pride for the entire family.

> SIMON HAYWARD WAS DRIVEN BY TWO FIRM PRINCIPLES — HONOUR AND DUTY.

Opposite: *Simon Hayward, a guardian of the Queen and part of the military elite, was an unlikely drugs-runner. He was, it seems, framed by his own brother.*

Below: *Simon Hayward freed from prison is embraced by the women who believe in his innocence, his fiancée, Sandra Agar on the left and his mother.*

The same values were shared by his elder brother David. But the same could not be said of Christopher, the black sheep of the family, whose devotion seemed to be only to himself and his hedonistic ways. In 1968 he left school after a dismal performance where he was constantly compared

unfavourably with his brothers. The Sixties, with its revolution in dress, music and taste, claimed Christopher. He became enmeshed in eastern philosophy and religion and a devotee of the mind-altering drugs espoused by many disciples of this 'alternative' lifestyle. Like many of his generation, who questioned the rigidity of the class system they were brought up in, he decided to go off in search of himself on the hippy trail to the Far East.

Christoper journeyed through Afghanistan, Thailand, India, becoming lost in clouds of smoke from marijuana that was plentiful and cheap. In 1971 his wanderings took him to Ibiza, the Spanish Balearic island that still retained its peace and charm; it had not yet been invaded by the hotel developers who would destroy much of its old world beauty. In Ibiza, Christopher fell in with a hippy crowd in the village of Santa Gertrudis, later moving to San Carlos on a remote headland where

SIMON HAS ALWAYS MAINTAINED THAT HE KNEW NOTHING ABOUT HIS BROTHER'S NEFARIOUS ACTIVITIES.

he bought a fishing boat and earned a few pesetas ferrying tourists through the crystal clear Mediterranean waters. With a plentiful supply of cheap hashish from Morocco that was landed in secret coves and inlets, Christopher had his own chunk of paradise far away from the rigidity of his upbringing in chilly England.

While Simon trained hard, he always had time to keep in touch with Christopher by mail. Although the brothers were, on the face of it, as different as chalk and cheese, they had a genuine affection for each other. From Ibiza, Christopher wrote to tell him that he had fallen in love with a hippy friend, a Swiss-born upper-crust young girl named Chantal Heubi. At twenty-two, she had also turned her back on the conventional life. Christopher explained to his brother how Chantal had lost their unborn baby the previous spring. It had devastated her at the time but further cemented the bond between the couple.

On 12 August 1972, he came back to London from Ibiza with her and married Chantal at Fulham register office – an occasion none of the officials forgot in a hurry as both bride and groom donned flowing red robes as favoured by members of the Bhagwan cult of eastern mysticism. The marriage lasted for two years during which time she produced a son, Tarik, by Christopher. Although they parted, they remained on good terms.

A BREAK IN THE SUN

The baby would later play a major part in the destruction of Simon Hayward.

While Christopher continued his lotus-eating lifestyle in sunny Ibiza, Christopher plunged into an army career. His talents marked him out for service with the Special Air Services Regiment, the feared and famed SAS, in Northern Ireland. In long, covert tours of duty in the bandit-ridden border country of Armagh he waged the war against the terrorists that his training had equipped him for. Every man in his unit knew what the IRA did if they captured an SAS man. Both sides played for keeps and the strain of duty told on every man. In March 1987 he felt it was time for a holiday and what better place to spend it than with his brother in the sunshine of the Mediterranean on the island of Ibiza?

Within days, Simon was lazing in the sunshine, drinking by the poolside while he stored up his energy for nights in the discos. Tourism had come with a vengeance now to Ibiza. After nearly two decades living there Christopher Hayward classified himself a native as much as anyone. He had learned Spanish, bought a bigger boat for tourist excursions and had invested in some property. He drove a Jaguar, a luxurious symbol of success.

But did Simon Hayward really know then what the police in Sweden would later allege he knew? That his brother used his catamaran Truelove for more than innocent excursions; that, in fact, he was a key member of an international drug smuggling cartel that bought top grade cannabis in Morocco? That he regularly sailed to Moroccan ports to pick up the consignments? That the drugs were then processed somewhere on mainland Spain before being distributed across Europe?

Simon has always maintained that he knew nothing about his brother's nefarious activities. But Interpol certainly did know and, if Captain Hayward has been telling the truth, he became caught like a fly in a spider's web that he never saw.

Simon was relaxing on holiday but eighteen hundred miles away in Sweden's second city, Uppsala, a high-level meeting between drugs squad officers in the city police and a drugs task force in the capital

Left: *The home of Hayward in Walton Street, London. It is the address of a man who had no need to indulge in squalid drug deals.*

Below: *The Jaguar that Hayward drove as a favour for his brother, Christopher. The car was packed with illegal substances.*

resin, destined for the students of Uppsala. Again the question must be asked: did Simon know when he made the offer what was in the car's fake panels or was he an innocent 'mule' whom the organisation was willing to sacrifice if things went wrong?

If Simon Hayward thought the instructions for the rendezvous with the man he was to contact in Sweden regarding the sale of the car bordered on the dramatic, he did not say so. His brother told him to drive to the railway station of the lonely town of Linkoping, one hundred and twenty miles from Stockholm, where he would meet a man called Lokesh.

Sure enough, at 10pm on 13 March, after a journey that had taken him across the continent, he met Lokesh who climbed

was taking place. They met to discuss the details of a two-year operation planned to smash the international drugs syndicate of which Christopher Hayward was part.

Uppsala, an old academic town with a five-thousand-strong university population eager to get its hands on cheap narcotics, had been the target for large-scale drug peddling by the syndicate. Intelligence told narcotic squads that the next consignment was due in March. Christopher Hayward had been under intense surveillance for months, but there were still no clues as to how the drugs might be couriered into the country. As these officers discussed the fine-tuning of the drugs bust, Christopher put a proposal to Simon his brother.

Midway through the first week of March he was joined in Ibiza by Sandra Agar, his beautiful society girlfriend from London, who was there to hear the proposition put to Simon. Christopher said he wanted to sell his British Racing Green Jaguar XJ6 because it was unsuitable for the winding, narrow roads of Ibiza. He said he had a buyer ready for it in Sweden and would Simon mind driving it to that country as part of his holiday?

Simon jumped at the offer, relishing the prospect of enjoying driving the high-performance car through some of the loveliest scenery in Europe. It was, of course, the car in which Christopher Hayward would plant one hundred and eleven pounds of cannabis

Above: *A good-looking and dashing young army officer, Simon Hayward was also a great party-goer. Before his arrest in Sweden, he was at a ball with Susan, left, and Tracey Woodall.*

Above, top: *Simon Hayward with Sandra Agar, the woman who loves him and believes him. She is convinced he was part of a ghastly frame-up.*

into the front seat of his car. Lokesh was a hippy name that the man had adopted on the island as part of the drug culture he was involved with. In reality he was Scottish-born Forbes Cay Mitchell, a man whom Simon had met briefly once on the island; a veteran drug smuggler who was assigned to get the car to the safe house where other syndicate members would strip it of the drugs. Simon Hayward still maintains he was, as far as he knew, taking the car to be sold. After that he would return to England and his regiment. But he would see neither again for several years. As they drove to the safe house they were arrested by Swedish police who had been planning the bust for nearly two years.

It did not take the police long to locate the drugs. First the elegant Jaguar was weighed and its manufacturer's weight compared with the police scale. It was found to be about one hundred and eleven pounds heavier, and it didn't take long to find the drugs hidden in secret panels in the doors; bag after bag of drugs was laid out on the floor of the Swedish police garage.

Pictures taken of Simon Hayward at the time and that appeared in British newspapers certainly conveyed the impression of a man in total shock, unable to believe what had happened to him. He protested his innocence and told police the whole story as he knew it. He vehemently denied being a drug runner and having anything to do with drugs at all. He was, he said, set up, and once his brother realised the predicament he was in he would step forward to clear his name. Five years on, he is still waiting for that to happen.

DABBLING IN A DANGEROUS GAME

Jan-Erik Nilson is a towering giant of a man, a police officer over six-foot six-inches tall, who, with prosecutor Ulf Forsberg, assembled the case against Simon Hayward. He briefed journalists assembled in Uppsala to cover the story of the shamed soldier with the following story. Cay Mitchell, Nilson said, had squealed on Christopher Hayward while in custody and explained why his brother was chosen to drive the drugs into Sweden. Cay Mitchell said that it was usually a man called Macundo who delivered the illegal cargoes, but his nerves were gone. Significantly, Cay Mitchell said that Simon Hayward knew what he was bringing in, that he was excited by the prospects of dabbling in such a dangerous game and that he was due for a handsome, unspecified reward for his efforts. 'He knew what he was doing,' said Nilson. 'We believe that Captain Hayward entered into this conspiracy willingly. He was not an innocent dupe in our opinion.'

Simon pinned his hopes on Christopher contacting him. Courageously and honourably, he refused to disown his brother even though it seemed, to those who believed his story, that he had been the vic-

> 'WE BELIEVE THAT CAPTAIN HAYWARD ENTERED INTO THIS CONSPIRACY WILLINGLY. HE WAS NOT AN INNOCENT DUPE IN OUR OPINION.'

tim of a frame-up. Police said they hoped to make contact with Christopher, believing that he might want to cut some sort of deal for leniency. If he held the key to identifying the top men of the syndicate, it would have gone a long way into getting a reduced sentence for both brothers. But by the time that his brother had been thrown to the police Christopher was already on the run; a price had been put on his head by the syndicate bosses who believed he had botched the job.

A newspaper has since confirmed that while Interpol was searching for Christopher, he had docked Truelove, his fifty-seven-foot catamaran, in M'diq, scene of so many of his illicit deals. Here he had a secret re-union with his son Tarik. The

Above: *A grim-faced Simon Hayward is driven off to begin a five-year sentence for a crime he protests he did not commit.*

love of his son convinced him that he could not help his brother. Christopher had been told that Tarik would be murdered if he cut any kind of deal with prosecutors in Sweden. Later, Christopher phoned his mother in England. He said he was sorry for what was happening to Simon, but that if he came forward to speak he would be killed and so would Tarik, and he said he was not prepared to let that happen. He was sorry for Simon, but that was the it was. Tarik meant more than Simon.

Cay Mitchell got seven years. At his trial he once again reiterated what he had already told police under interrogation: that Simon Hayward knew everything about the drug running operation and that he was an enthusiastic collaborator in it. Things looked bleak for the disgraced officer at his trial.

His lawyers emphasised the fact that Hayward had never been in trouble before and was merely helping his brother out when he agreed to drive his car. But why, then, asked the judges, was the rendezvous with this car buyer in the car park of a lonely railway station at the dead of night? How come the screwdriver which fitted into the specially-designed holes securing the hollowed out door panel was inside the car? Surely the good Captain must have known of this? What about an overheard conversation that Cay Mitchell alleged Simon had with his brother in which he jumped at the chance to courier the drugs into Sweden? The only defence Simon had, and which he maintains to this day, is that he was tricked by someone he believed in absolutely. While the court recognised his excellent career, his unblemished character and his stoic defence of his brother, it nevertheless found him Guilty and sentenced him to five years.

Below: *Simon Hayward published a book about his ordeal. There is still no trace of the whereabouts of his brother, Christopher, who seems to have been responsible for his brother Simon's arrest and imprisonment.*

Events after he was sentenced cast an even more favourable light upon his plea of innocence. Shortly before the verdict in July, Christopher's ex-wife Chantal telephoned Mrs Hayward at her London home. Mrs Hayward, who had lost her husband, one son in jail and the other on the run, was astonished to hear her claim that she had evidence who was behind the drugs run. She told her that it was neither Christopher nor Simon. She refused to reveal the name over the phone but promised to fly to London from Ibiza to speak with solicitors. Mrs Hayward urged her to make the journey as soon as possible but just days before she was scheduled to arrive she was found dead with a needle in her arm.

THE RIGHT-HAND TURNS SINISTER

An autopsy showed that she had died from heroin and other drugs mixed together in a lethal cocktail. But Chantal's friends all knew her as a woman who had dabbled in marijuana but had never, ever fallen into hard drug use. And more mysterious was the fact that the needle was plunged into her left arm even though she was left-handed. It begged the question: why did a girl unused to injecting drugs use an unfamiliar hand to do so? Her death coming just days before she was due to arrive in London led Simon's supporters to believe the poor woman had been murdered.

A court has to prove guilt 'beyond reasonable doubt'. Simon Hayward continues to maintain his innocence, even though his sentence is behind him. He does not know of the whereabouts of his brother, or even if he is still alive. But the ingrained decency in Simon Hayward has given way to a bitterness towards the brother who condemned him to a prison term. He says: 'Ninety-nine per cent of me believes that Christopher stitched me up. Only that other one per cent clings to the fact that he is my brother, that he couldn't have done. But ninety-nine per cent screams out that he did. One thing is very obvious. Whether he did or he didn't, whether he is genuinely terrified of something or somebody that I know nothing about, there must have been some way for him to get a message or information through to clear me. He has not done that and for that I will never forgive him.' But where is Christopher?